Love a Boll Weevil

And Other Lessons God Taught Me

Bonnye Matthews

Printed in the United States of America.

ISBN 978-1-954896-29-1 paperback

ISBN 978-1-954896-31-4 hardbound

ISBN 978-1-954896-30-7 ebook

Library of Congress Control Number: 2025911554

Fathom Publishing Company
Anchorage, Alaska
fathompublishing.com
booksbybonnye.com

Boll Weevil Backstory

God brought me an overpowering vision when I was six. I was shown things God wanted me to learn. One lesson was that loving the lovable required nothing from one who loves. Loving the unlovable—that requires care from the love giver. It is something asked of Christians.

I walked through a cotton field and noticed a boll weevil. They were bizarre bugs to me. I compared them to another funny-looking bug, the praying mantis, two odd-looking bugs. I knew boll weevils had destroyed the cotton crops on which farmers in the South depended in 1915.

Boll weevils were despised for decades amid attempts to eradicate them. People called them evil weevils. They weren't evil. They were just living as they were designed to live.

In Alabama, some people looked beyond the odd-looking, seemingly evil aspects of boll weevils. Instead of hate, they were moved eventually to love. They learned the boll weevil's message—diversification.

The farmers learned to mix what they planted and not depend on a single crop. They learned to add manufacturing to their income-producing work. The citizens benefited from the boll weevils' lessons. Where other southern areas were struggling with eradicating these bugs, one city—Enterprise, Alabama—even raised a memorial to the boll weevil in 1919 due to their financial success following the boll weevil's lesson of diversification.

Love the unlovable and you may find the blessing it brings.

Dedication

Katharine Bradley was my spiritual mentor throughout my life.

I dedicate this book to my great-aunt Katy. When I was a small child Katy taught me Bible stories, explained to me the parts of the church building, let me know that the sanctuary was a special place where in reverence people were quiet and still while they met with a holy God to worship Him. She explained to me what holy meant.

Katy also played the piano and taught me hymns for children. She explained with care why I needed Jesus, and helped me memorize the responses to the questions in the Westminster Catechism for Children.

Katy was a woman who never had children, but she loved little ones and was graced with patience and understanding of the psyche of a child. She wanted to share what she knew of the Bible. She answered my questions when I had them. I absorbed the information as a parched land absorbs slow rain.

Unbeknownst to Katy, her teaching brought me into contact with the spiritual world. She didn't have spiritual encounters in life. Her words meant one thing to her cognitively and something in a spiritual world came through to me. Both of us experienced spiritual understanding, but our routes to get there differed.

From what she taught me, I could exist in the physical world and the spiritual world, while she remained in the physical world. To her, talking with God meant prayer; to me, talking with God meant talking with Him as I talked with people, only applied to an invisible God whom I could hear or understand in different ways.

The word spiritual has a few meanings. Used here Webster defines it as "of, relating to, consisting of, or affecting the spirit: INCORPOREAL," as opposed to "of or relating to sacred matters," as Webster describes spiritual songs. My experience would be the sense of "in the spirit" as used in parts of the Bible describing human behavior in a different dimension, such as Moses encountering God as fire in a bush. God was different from Katy in that He is Creator, Perfect Love, Truth, and invisible. She was like me, human.

I understood those things at the age of three because I talked to God as well as Katy. God in the form of Father can make representations of Himself as if He were visible. I cannot see Him, because He is spirit unless He forms Himself into a visible being. He communicates through talking, impressing something upon me, providing dreams or visions. God, the Son, can appear to us as He did to His followers after arising from death. God the Holy Spirit is one I've never seen represented visually.

Katy devoured Christian books. Whereas my entry into the spiritual world followed from my craving to know God personally, I expected that was normal. No one ever told me it wasn't. Katy's teaching me was thorough basic information on what I needed to know, but it was God who chose to bring me into the spiritual world with teaching from a spiritual dimension. Katy got her information from researching the Bible and books.

I couldn't read the books Katy could when I was three. When I was in my late sixties, Katy asked me why I thought God talked to me and not her. My reply was that I likely needed it, when she didn't. I was little. I couldn't read. And, if I wanted to know something I'd ask questions of people and God, and if I didn't understand, I'd pursue God with all my effort. Also, Katy had taught me that God was invisible. I met Him. I talked to Him. No one ever said He didn't talk back. He did, and so our communication began.

I was introduced to my heavenly Father at age three and I believed. I don't have a pin pointed day I became Christian. I knew who God was, why I needed Jesus, and I knew His love and was utterly, magnetically drawn to Him. Does the Bible say any of that somewhere? I can't find it expressed that way. I can't find "accepting Him into my heart" either. I expected and felt God's presence in the sanctuary clearly and with joy. I recognized He was alive, He talked with me, and best of all, He loved me. He was in my small view of things present with His holy love invisible. I can affirm that I was His even then.

In the sanctuary, it seemed to me that I could snuggle against our great and wonderful God while the service occurred or meeting took place, soaking up His immensity and being close to One who was not like me. Someone special and holy—so different. To me, holy implied that He knew all things all the time; having strength over all the universe, which I saw then as the earth where I lived and all that I could see with my eyes in the night sky. I had no sense at that time of what little we can see in the night sky. Holy implied being filled with a love greater than I could imagine. Holy is being set aside for all that is good; nothing bad. I could certainly feel it.

I wanted to know more of Him. A lot more. I suppose I was a pest about it. Oddly, both my heavenly Father and Katy seemed happy to share with me and answer endless questions. It was edifying and joyful. His differences attracted me as strongly as the refrigerator door drew my little felt-covered magnet. When I wanted to think, I tossed a tiny magnet at the refrigerator door at home. I watched as the magnet made a strong leap to the refrigerator as if it were driven by greater speed at a certain closeness to stick to that refrigerator door. His draw to me was magnetic. And from both God and Katy that magnetism gave me knowledge and took place in a surrounding of joy.

Acknowledgments

To pull this book together, help came from the following:

Randy Matthews

Rebecca A. Goodrich

Alice Cudlipp

Magdel Roets

Sally Sutherland

Cathy Boehling

Rob Bignell

Valton Herman

Jacqui Scherrer

Elena Hartwell/Allegory Editing

Constance Taylor

Teena Helmericks

Emelia Barquet

Jon Sneed

Contents

Boll Weevil Backstory   iii

Dedication   v

Acknowledgments   ix

Contents   xi

Note to the Reader   xiii

Revelation in a Parking Lot   1

Holy Disobedience   5

In the Sanctuary   9

The Vision   13

Finding His Pocket   19

Love a Boll Weevil   23

Never Poke Around   27

Part of the Body of Christ   29

Anole and Disbelief   33

Holy Eyes   39

MtDNA and Healing   43

Lion of Judah   47

Preparing to Prepare for Work   51

College Days   55

The Unforgivable Sin   65

Teaching   67

Becoming Mom   73

Heavy, Heavy, Heavy Air   77

What We're Designed For?   81

Dad Sees Angels   85

Flashlight   89

Explode?   91

Crazy or True   93

Quicksand at the Toutle River   95

Blake Barrett—Tempting Satan   99

Crossing Chasms   101

Shower of Roses   111

Demon   119
Weeping Whales   121
Neuropsychological Exam and a Toad   125
Georgia Hamilton and the Angels   127
Nyla, Huge Lesson   131
Essential Epitome of Equality   135
Porcupine and the Laugh of God   139
Restoration   143
Afterword   147
About the Author   151

Note to the Reader

Love a Boll Weevil is a memoir based on my memories and research. The purpose of this book is to share my walk with God, to share what my spiritual life has been like.

Lacking a complete recording of the past, I have tried to re-create events, locales, and conversations from my recollections. I have changed the names of most individuals and places, some identifying characteristics, and details such as physical appearances, occupations, and places of residence. I have re-created dialogue, intending to convey the message and tone of each conversation if not the actual words.

Other people have said that I am "different." I agree. I live with one foot in the physical world with logical, scientific analysis and the other in the world of the spirit with rock solid faith. Some might consider me a type of mystic. I define mystic as a way of being, not doing: having a spiritual openness to the sovereignty of God and His wisdom, living a God-dependent life, describing life as "walking with God," but that's not exactly how it goes. It includes a waiting on the Lord for what He would have me do or hear, definitely not running about trying to figure out how to please Him. I have spent my life waiting on Him to lead me.

I can be in either the spiritual or the physical world or both at the same time. A few have argued with me that being in both places—physical and spiritual—at the same time is impossible. It is possible for me.

I'm the happiest person I have ever known, not crazy, just genuinely happy to have my life the way it is. Those so-called opposites merge into a singleness in me where instead of stress from things that fail to fit together, they not only fit together but also, they smooth out the controversies and stresses for me, so I can see more clearly. It provides cohesion.

People ask me what church I attend and when I first took Jesus into my heart. My answer gets a strange reaction, but my answer is "I take the church with me wherever I go." The church is the body of Christ on this earth, and of that I am a part. I find nowhere in scripture that I'm supposed to take Jesus into my heart. I am to believe that Jesus's substitutionary death on the cross is payment for my salvation from sin.

I've included information details that demonstrates how God has worked in my life to assure that I learned what He wants me to know. Being a kid in a military family, the idea of a special cradle-to-grave church, where one develops spiritually, was not part of my world. God took on the role of growing me in the spiritual world from age five, though as to why, I have no clue. He didn't choose to teach me because I'm a good candidate or deserving in any way. I've been the complete reverse of a meritorious choice, having more than occasionally asked Him whether He'd lost His mind. He never tells me to do something that I think of as something I want to do or I find wise in human terms. That shows my poverty of wisdom, not His.

Dear Reader, please don't compare your life with mine.* Each of us is different by design. We are called to different purposes and dealt with in different ways. We are gifted and helped along the way by our needs and God's purposes. I suggest that you follow God. Get to know Him. Do His bidding. When you are God's, no one else can set a pattern for your life. When you follow His pattern, you are extraordinarily blessed while not heavily burdened.

Bonnye Matthews
Mat-Su Borough, Alaska
In the Year of Our Lord, 2025

---

*   II Corinthians 10:12

Revelation in a Parking Lot

I was six when God told me He had something He wanted me to do for Him, but He didn't say what it was. I was in my seventies sitting in my car in this parking lot with the lovely view when I learned. He wanted me to write a book about our shared experience. Truly, it was easier, I learned, not to know my assignment!

In the parking lot at a large grocery in Palmer, Alaska, I was irritated at the weakness that my old age presented. I positioned with great effort a heavy case of paper from the cart into my van and tossed a bag of ink cartridges on top. I tipped my rolling walker and guided it into the side of the van.

There were picturesque mountains to the east and south of me. These mountains had been raised from the sea floor to tower over the valley forming a barrier between me and the Pacific Ocean. The lovely or unique in nature usually sang a siren song to me, but not this day. Normally, nature would be my first focus. But instead, I slid into the driver's seat, poked the door lock button, and reached for the seat belt.

Simultaneously, I was busy with the draw of my Father's spiritual world. I'd been able to enter the spiritual world either through my choice or through summons for many decades. But this day, I was drawn by what I call a spiritual snare which tugged at me irresistibly.

My body remained in the car, but my spirit left it. I had no idea where we were. A room somewhere? Somewhere in the spirit world?

Instantly, I was in communication with my Father. My eyes were open, but my vision was limited, I focused totally on Him. The visual space was cataract-vision, dark and foggy. His presence added the only light which brightened the scene significantly but did not make it clearer. My usually clear spiritual eyes were cloudy.

A head formed in the fog much like the bust statuary of antiquity. As the fog cleared and the head came into focus, hideous deformities became visible. The bust was my head, neck, and shoulders. The skin above my ears was swollen like too much belly fat overhanging blue jeans—a monstrous hat of fat on my head. I watched it jiggle and was brought to the edge of nausea. I was horrified at what I saw.

"What happened to my head?" I whispered.

"It's a representation."

"What?"

"You could say it shows your spiritual obesity from never sharing our journey. The purpose of your learning is to share what you learn. You know that."

A memory from age three leapt into my mind. I recalled the day when I learned Mom didn't consider that today's people walked with God. She thought that was only for a few special people long ago in the Bible. Certainly not something I could do. In a toughened voice, she insisted that I stop pretending such things. I refused to give up my time with God. I continued but hid my time with God from everyone, even Katy. I wasn't pretending.

"Your failure to share was acceptable in the past. But for many, many years you've wanted to know what assignment I had for you."

It struck me—He'd said something about the assignment He had for me to do.

"Indeed, Father, I've wanted to know. I've waited for over seven decades." My excitement grew. Would I learn now?

"Now," He said. "It's time."

After waiting for so long, I was surprised. After all these years, He'd finally tell me what I was born to do. My excitement grew.

"Write the story of your spiritual journey with Me. Write a book so others may share your time with Me and some of what we discussed."

This struck me speechless. Had He told me to light myself afire, I could not have been any more shocked. What He asked me to do carried crushing responsibility. The book would have to be as perfect as possible. Utter truth. There was no video of my life I could refer to. No journals existed. Before moving to Alaska, I'd shredded the few that I had. I had nothing to help me with details. I was sinking in on myself, overwhelmed, daunted. Non-verbal.

"I waited to tell you until now," my Father said, "because had you known, it would have influenced your choices in life, turning you into someone you aren't."

I laughed, lightening up for the first time since He told me my assignment. "I might have been a lot easier for You to deal with."

"I chose you as you are, not as you think I might want you to be."

That gave me something to ponder. "Lord, if I were to write down this whole spiritual journey, it would take volumes."

"Share what you remember. Share what was important to you."

"Okay." I could think of nothing else to say. What a job! Never in my life had I been so bewildered. Rational organization was one of my strong points, but this left me with no clue how to begin.

He put His hand on my shoulder. "You can do it. I'm pleased with your book."

With those words, I could see the book forming from the fog—the book I was going to write. My vision wasn't clear, but I could see part of the image. There was earth color on the cover.

"Sharing this experience will bring the vision of your obese head down to a normal size for you'll lose much of what you've carried alone all these years. It's time to let it out. Have no fear."

I sat and melted into that lovely spiritual silence that I could share with Him. As with many other times, my spirit size literally grew fast during spiritual encounters, exceeding my physical size while taking in spiritual things. I needed time to find normal again, to decompress and return my spirit to physical size. No longer could I be angry knowing He had something for me to do, but not knowing what it was. Now I knew, and it overpowered me. We spoke a little longer about nothings as my physical and spiritual size returned to their proper dimensions.

As I merged back into the physical world, I recalled my earlier purchase and, in a release of tension, laughed and laughed. I had certainly made the right purchase, computer printer paper and ink. I couldn't have imagined learning my assignment this way in a parking lot! Now, after more than seven and a half decades, I knew.

Fully back to the physical world, I belted up, and turned the key in the ignition. I wondered how I could even begin this work.

Holy Disobedience

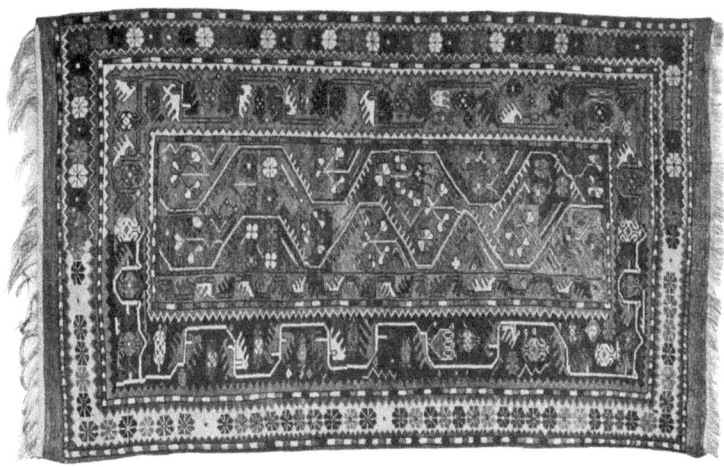

The old Oriental rug common to homes in the nineteen forties. Red was a common basic color. They provided a place for children to play and kept down some of the coal dust that accumulated from the main source of heat which could rise with a breeze to make people cough.

I experienced a serious shock one day in my third year of life as I conversed with my heavenly Father.

Mom asked, "Bonnye who are you talking to?"

Half attentive, I replied, "God."

"You mean you're praying?"

"No, we're just talkin'."

Mom's face clouded. "What do you mean talking?"

"Talkin' like you and I talk."

Mom leaned down a little, hovering over me. One hand held a dish towel. She seated that hand on her hip. "You hear Him talk to you?"

"Of course." Didn't she?

Mom drilled her eyes into mine. "He's not answering you like we do, right? He doesn't talk to people today. He did that a long,

long time ago, back in Bible times. We have the Bible so He has no need to spend His time talking to us directly." She made it sound as if talking with us was a burden for Him.

I looked up in shock. How do I answer that? I put my hands flat on the floor to sit up straighter, pushing my back against the wall. My hands were half on the rug and half off. I could feel the ancient fringed uneven border where sections of fringe were missing from wear at the rug's edge. It was a tired, busily-designed, faded red rug common at that time. Its usefulness was that it helped to hold the coal dust down inside the house. I lived in Richmond, Virginia where the common source of heat was coal. Coal dust collected everywhere.

Mom stooped down a lot nearer to my level. She was very serious. I thought she'd be happy with my explanation when she asked who I spoke to. She responded in what I suspected was horror. Her forehead formed a wrinkled V. I didn't understand her reaction at all.

Her forehead furrowed deeper, still holding the shape of a V. "You must stop this talking with God right now." Her voice was firmer and louder.

"But-but," I stammered, "people walk with God. You don't walk with God and not talk."

"What are you talking about?" She didn't understand why I couldn't easily comply.

In that moment, I detached from God. I couldn't talk to her and my Father at the same time. "Because . . . 'cause . . . 'cause," I stammered. "Enoch walked with God!" I turned defensive, pulling on my feeble power to raise my voice. I didn't think she knew what she was asking. I certainly didn't know how to answer her.

"That was a very long time ago, and you're not like Enoch." She grew louder and more forceful. "You are to do what I tell you to do. You are to stop this time you think you spend with God right now. You're treating God like your imaginary dog."

I looked at her with tears in my eyes. She really didn't talk with God? She knew what He had to say about children and obedience, but not other things? How could she not talk with Him? But this was not the time to question her. Silence was called for. I gazed at my lap.

With mature eyes later in life, I suspected that she was doing what many Christians did at that time. She went to church on Sundays. She listened to the sermon. She learned. But it wasn't deep spiritually. She may have thought that's all there was. As a child who experienced spiritual things, I definitely didn't understand. I didn't know the term spiritual for what I experienced. To me talking with God was a normal part of life, a part I loved. The best part. I couldn't understand Mom's reaction, so I remained silent. I used my fingers to comb through the pathetic rug fringe. At the same time, I pitied Mom. It was probably the first time in my life that I ever felt pity for an adult. How could she not know? How could she miss the best part of life? Did something happen when people got old?

As she continued to berate me, I shrank along the wall. My tears fell. I nodded, looking into her eyes. She must've taken my nod as agreement, but I was only answering that I understood. She got up and walked back to rejoin my great-grandmother Neenee, expecting obedience from me.

I was taught from an early age to reason. So, I did. God made the rules. My time with God was clearly okay with Him. He participated! If it were okay with Him, how could it not be okay with my mother? Consequently, I continued my walking with God, but as a close-held secret that I shared with no one. Not even Katy.

After childhood, I continued the secret from habit, not need. For seventy-some years, I spoke to absolutely no one about my walking and talking with God, except one other person who lived a similar dual life between the physical and spiritual worlds. The one person with whom I shared was Georgia Hamilton and we were overjoyed to find each other. I was in my thirties. She was older. To know someone else understood what my spiritual life was like was encouraging. We could share.

Ultimately my choice to continue with God but hide that time resulted in a type of rightdoing instead of wrongdoing. As a little child, I called the action I took with Mom holy disobedience. I didn't know holy disobedience was already a thing—a different thing. Holy disobedience meant civil disobedience or an action for religious use.

In my mind, it meant choosing to believe God. He was a good and constant guide.

In the Sanctuary

My first church was Westminster Presbyterian Church on Park Avenue in Richmond, Virginia. It is where I first met God and began my time of getting to know Him.

"YES! NO! YES! NO! YES! NO! YES! NO!" I shouted echoing the vote counters at the top of my lungs in the sanctuary of the old Westminster Presbyterian Church. I stomped on the pew, up near the front, where I'd abandoned my seated position. I knew I shouldn't stand on pews. It was superbly the wrong thing to do. I was, however, on my feet before I realized it. I was four years old. Every cell in my little body was super charged.

The ladies were dressed in their special church frocks, some polka dotted on a background of mostly dark navy or a bit lighter solid blue. The scent of their dry cleaned clothes burned my eyes. There were gentlemen in tired wool suits, which sported shiny spots of wear, giving off the same pungent dry cleaner fumes. They sat at the table between the altar and pews on the left side as we faced front. These Yes/No people cast glares of disapproval at me, but I didn't care.

Katy swiftly picked me up and took me to the vestibule, where she bent down to my level and asked, "Bonnye, what on earth is the matter with you?"

Tears streaked my face. I could hardly speak.

"What is it?" Katy inquired with understanding and great patience.

"They are makin' silly noise in the sanctuary. That's not rev'rence."

"Honey, they are counting the votes to decide whether to sell this church building." She'd already told me what would happen at church that night.

"They are in the sanctuary," I stuttered out one word at a time, horrified. I felt as if "in the sanctuary" explained it all. Katy had carefully taught me correct sanctuary behavior. What the adults were doing wasn't it. It wasn't reverent, and it wasn't quiet. They weren't worshipping God. Some of the adults were furious with others. They didn't try to control themselves.

Katy struggled to understand my upset. I tried to explain. A door on the side of the sanctuary led to a smaller room. I reasoned they could go through that door and Yes/No in there so as not to disturb our holy God. It was okay to talk in that other room, even talk loudly. I felt they should do their silly Yes/No there. God was holy. Yes/No was not! I couldn't figure out how to express what was disturbing me. Katy tried to calm me with a gentle touch to my arm, but it didn't work. Katy wiped my tears.

"They laugh out loud! And yell at each other. They make a lot of noise. In the sanctuary. And God is here. Don't they know God is here? God is holy!" I pronounced holy in a whisper, as if the actual word were holy. To me, it was. Katy had poured her teaching into a receptive vessel. Those words became part of me. I never had questioned her in godly things. Katy finally understood. She was hearing a replay of her teaching.

"If church people want to know whether to sell the church, why don't they just ask God?"

As an old woman today, I can smile at that. Katy later admitted that she was so shocked because she didn't know how to handle my question. She could understand how all I'd been taught had turned the sanctuary into something like the Old Testament Holy of Holies, though she'd never introduced that term let alone idea to me.

By that age, I both loved and feared God. What would He do about this unholy loud noise in His holy place? If a lightning bolt had pierced the roof of the church building and landed at our feet, I wouldn't have been surprised. I knew about Moses and the burning bush and Samson destroying a church of a pagan god. When God was there, the very ground was holy. Things could happen. Frightening things.

Later I learned that I had made Katy wonder for the first time whether the vote counting was appropriate in the sanctuary. The meeting of deacons, elders, and the congregation that evening was conducted as Presbyterians conduct congregational meetings—in the sanctuary. Deacons and Elders would have presented the data; there would have been discussion; the people would have voted.

In my little mind, the congregational meeting was out of place in the sanctuary. To tell a child they must be silent and still in that room, and then display a divided group of people vigorously discussing a serious matter, loudly and with gesticulations, flew in the face of what I had been taught about that room. In my own way, I wanted to shield God from the noise and movement but didn't know how. My respect for adults was shattered.

While I waited in the vestibule, Katy returned to gather our things from the pew. While the Yes/No sounds still filled the air, Katy came back and helped me into my matching leggings, coat, and bonnet and we headed home.

Katy explained to me that sometimes adults forget and do what they tell little people not to do. That helped my view of adults. They could do wrong things too. It was a fleeting moment of enlightenment. Katy never would have pretended to me that the voting behavior was okay in the sanctuary, based on what she knew she'd carefully taught me.

As we walked home, Katy helped me get past my trauma by talking about various things we saw along the way. She was holding my hand on one side of me, and the Lord was literally holding my other hand. My world was good again.

The Vision

I was just five years old when Dad transferred to Bossier City, Louisiana, and we left everything I knew behind in Richmond. Dad, a fully-fledged pilot in the US Air Force, piloted B-29s, a huge propeller-driven workhorse of an airplane. I'd just finished my first year in kindergarten at Pleasant Heart Elementary School in Shreveport across the Red River from Bossier City.

School changed things. I slipped from a person living with one foot in the everyday world and the other in the spiritual world to one living totally in the everyday world. Gradually, all the changes in my life took over the routine I had established, and they kept me busy with things connected to new places, school, making friends. I was learning an entirely different way of life without Katy. I was so busy with all the gradual changes that I hardly noticed the lack of my spiritual walks.

In June, I heard a car drive up our driveway. I ran from the backyard to the front of the house. I knew Dad was returning from England, and sure enough, a blue-suited military guy let Dad off. Dad picked up his bags as I rounded the house only to put them back down as I flew at him, arms wide out to my sides for a hug. Mom opened the front door as Dad spun around holding me high in the air. He put me down, and I went to find Randy.

The four of us gathered in the living room. Dad said he had brought presents. Presents? Presents were for birthdays and Christmas. This was neither. From his largest bag, Dad pulled out a big book and laid it on the floor between Randy and me. It was *The Golden Bible*.

Instantly I felt a terrible pain in my belly. My eyes searched the room. It was as if an intruder had come among us. Quietly, like a snake. The invasion brought anxiety, and my excitement over Dad's return lost its edge. The book pointed to my loss, oversight, my inattention, what was missing in my life.

Silently, I cried out, "My Father! I forgot You! You are here. It makes me realize now that I have missed life with You."

Randy ran his little fingers over the cover. I didn't touch the book. I could feel the presence of God in the living room with me, but I was apparently the only one who knew He was there. His loving presence just filled the space for me.

He didn't appear angry that I'd forgotten Him. He seemed happy to see me. I had to control myself. Being with Him had to be secret which was hard. I was choked up with joy. I looked at the book. It seemed to feel less intimidatingly chockful of accusations, but my anxiety remained high. How could I have forgotten the most important person in my life?

Dad gave Mom a gift in a white box with gold writing on it and the number five. I had no idea what it was; my interest was focused on a child's book. I wanted to restart life with my wonderful God. But how?

When Mom finished hugging Dad for her gift and chatting with him in the kitchen, she called us to lunch. She'd made tomato soup and grilled cheese sandwiches cut into quarters on the diagonal as she always did. Dad removed his tie, unbuttoned his shirt, and tossed it onto the sofa, then kicked off his shoes. We went to eat.

"Hey, Little Girl," Dad said. "You're being awful quiet."

"Just glad you're home. Thank you for the book. I can hardly wait to read it."

"I hope you enjoy it. Oddly, the book was made in the United States, but I found it in England."

"That's far away." I shared my kindergarten knowledge. We had been taught a bit of geography.

"Yes, it is," Dad sighed.

I cleared the table.

"Is it okay if I take the book outside to read?" I asked.

"Take it anywhere you like. It's for you and Randy, but it'll be a few years before he's ready for it." Dad grinned, happy that I liked the book.

Immediately, I took *The Golden Bible* to the edge of the bayou which stretched beside our house situated north to south. When I sat on the dried brown grass, the stiff vegetation poked my bare legs. It was not at all comfortable. I wanted jeans like Randy had or long skirts like people wore long ago, but girls wore short dresses in 1948. Nevertheless, I intended to read the book by the bayou. The day was quiet, and the sun was behind me.

I laid the book across my legs. It was big, about ten by thirteen inches. I gazed off to the partly cloudy sky. The book had touched a super sensitive nerve that was beginning to calm. The last time I had talked with God was before kindergarten. Now I'd just finished that school year.

I whispered to Him and He was there.

"I forgot You. Oh, Lord, my God, I forgot You! I'm so sorry. Without Katy, I forgot."

"You can no longer depend on Katharine. You must find a way that causes you to remember the importance of seeking Me."

"Now it's my responsibility?"

"You begin to see."

"Please, stay close to me."

"Of course, for the rest of your life."

I opened the book, sensing it might help me remember that God matters. Stories Katy had taught me many times were there. I examined the pictures in detail. One of my favorites was "Jacob's Dream in the Desert" where the gates of heaven opened in golden glory with angels walking up and down the stairway. I couldn't count the times Katy had told me this story though she called it "Jacob's Ladder."

I could feel the Lord's presence and love as my heart went to Him. He was the same God I'd known for so long. He didn't change just because I had known Him in Virginia and now was with Him again in Louisiana.

The image in the book absorbed me. I read as well as I could, ignoring the tough words. Then, I stared at the picture. Something felt odd. The scent of roses came to me though there weren't any growing nearby.

I looked up and to my shock, golden stairs floated over the bayou. The stairs didn't look like metal but rather stones cut neatly. I thought that the golden sun reflected off a damp surface in the afternoon light. Later in memory, the stairs would strike me as damp rocks cut into rectangles. I had never thought of huge rocks cut into precise shapes. To me, rocks were formed in limitless shapes.

I was dumbstruck. How did He keep the stairs in the air? They looked heavy as if they should crash to the swampy bottom of the bayou. Never could I have imagined such a thing as He presented me that day. I stared at the sight for a long time, taking in every detail and absorbing the meaning it conveyed. The draw of the image over the bayou was much stronger than the pull of the magnet I tossed at the refrigerator door. I lost all consciousness of prickly grass. I had moved spiritually to the bottom of the stairs, while my physical body remained behind. Every cell in my being responded in joy. I wanted to run up the floating stairs, but I couldn't reach them.

I heard His words as if they came from afar. "This is made for you as an illustration of entry to heaven." I wondered whether I was about to die.

"It's not yet time for you to come here. You have many years to live first. I have a place for you when it is time. Your forever home will be here."

I had seen the movie Bambi, a cartoon. It was not like this. In front of my eyes was an amazing vision, though I had not heard that word used that way at the time. The story of Jacob's Ladder didn't connect with what I was seeing at that moment. This vision was made for me, not Jacob. Without questioning, I accepted it as "normal" for my time with God. He knew how to communicate to me. I'd recognize this place when I died and arrived at the gates of heaven. To "get it" close attention was necessary. I had to focus on all the details.

I had never seen anything so stupefying, so powerful. I'd had a concept of alive and not alive since early childhood. This was alive in a different way. The vision opened my understanding to different dimensions. It was alive in the spiritual dimension. I couldn't have used those words then though I recognized the difference. God was expanding my mind.

God doesn't teach like parents or schools teach. He provides an experience and the tools to figure out the lesson. He doesn't tell me what I'm supposed to learn. I have to learn it His way—by figuring it out with His guidance, immediately or over time in small bites.

I rested in Him to observe. My brain sometimes experienced wordless communication, eventually stored as words once I understood. Clearly God had shown me the spirit world that day.

The vision absorbed me. It was the experience; the book was the tool God used to introduce the vision.

The picture in the book drew on many things: memory of the stories Katy had told, my having just read the story and viewed the exquisite artwork. God pulled all these things together to show me this vision.

He decides whom to teach, when, how, and what as well as whether to teach at all. The student is simply the vessel to receive it. He intended for me to learn that He had a home for me.

Something else registered as I contemplated this experience. He had used the book. That meant He touched Dad in England to buy the book to bring home to us. That meant that God brought many things together so that He could create this event when it was time. He didn't live in time as I did, but He was able to work with time when He wanted.

I was filled with a non-verbal understanding of the beauty of God though I knew the image wasn't God Himself, but rather how He made Himself appear to me so that I could understand.

I wanted to go up those steps, ascending at a dead run, not caring what remained behind including family near and far, my school and friends, pets, things. I wanted to run up there to throw my arms around Him. But, it was a vision. God showed me that someday—someday I'd walk up steps like those to heaven, and He would be waiting for me.

"Father!" I said it loud enough for anyone nearby to hear. I'd forgotten momentarily that our talks were to be kept secret. I looked around.

"Father? Why me? I'm just a nobody kid. Why me?"

"I chose you. Not because you earned it or deserve it. But simply because I chose you. I have something I want you to do for me. You will do it. You and I will be glad you did. Your life is a chance for you to learn more. Your constant effort to come to know me in more depth is a small part of why I chose you. Beyond that, it is not for you to know why I chose you."

I looked down at the book and I looked back up, the vision faded and was soon gone. But *The Golden Bible* would keep the image alive for me. The art was only an approximation, but it would serve as a reminder.

I had progressed in age, and I felt God's presence more clearly than I had back in Virginia. That progress expanded my spirit, far larger than my physical self, and it helped me understand things I'd never imagined before. God had purpose for me here. The word destiny popped into my mind. I had a destiny.

All this and I was not in a sanctuary. I could come this close to God in places that were not the sanctuary! Places like the bayou. The strength of His holiness here with a vision and new understanding was powerful in the extreme to me. I suppose I already knew that since I loved outside time spent looking at what He created.

I remembered the story of the prodigal son. Breaking his father's heart, the son demanded his inheritance and left home. The son squandered his inheritance and ended up working as a servant for food. He finally returned home hoping to work for his father to earn his food. Instead of being angry, the prodigal's father celebrated the return of his son. The father didn't make a big deal out of his forgiveness. He forgave and moved on, not shaming his son. The father celebrated instead.

As I thought on this I realized that this experience of the prodigal was much like how God deals with humans. I saw the book and there was instant repentance. I had not sought God. He forgave my oversight and through Christ I was redeemed. I would use the book Dad had brought to help me stay close to God. I would never be alone, for God would teach me, and I would learn to be the me He wanted me to be.

God had made a home for me already. He said so. In that place I glimpsed over the bayou. I knew about rent and I wondered if I could afford it.

I could hear Him laugh.

"I made a place for you. It's a gift. There will be no rent."

He knew my thoughts, and He laughed. God laughing?—I thought that was wonderful. Sadly, there was no one with whom I could share that God laughed.

The sun was irritating my skin and I needed to cool down. I stood up with the book and headed across the street to a tree where shade would be plentiful.

Finding His Pocket

Dazed, I walked across the street to the cotton field to be in the cooling shade. I held the book tight to my chest, protecting the cover from sandpapery cotton bolls. Although they scratched my arms and legs, I didn't care. I walked slowly, thinking and marveling over the experience. I was submerged in the spiritual. If there were degrees of love, He must really love me. I knew I wasn't special, but God cared for me so much.

I walked through the cotton field, where I was allowed to play— but where no others were likely to be. I sat on a tree root and leaned against the tree, shaded by boughs thick with leaves, the book still clutched tightly to my chest behind my crossed arms.

A massive dose of humility and love fell upon me like a heavy cloud. I had feelings that I'd never had before, and they tumbled inside me as clothing did in an agitator washing machine. He knew me and loved me before I inhaled my first breath of air, even before He created the earth.*

God had given me a tiny clue today. He chose me in part because I wanted to know Him. He said it was time for me to remind myself to seek Him. Would this time with Him stop if I forgot Him again? I worried and made a pact with myself—I'd use the book as a reminder. I had to become more responsible.

However, He had also made it clear that He would be with me for the rest of my life. But yet, my forgetting Him again would not be okay. Not okay with whom? It wouldn't be okay with me. I was learning.

This taught me something about responsibility. I grasped the book tighter. He loved me even when I wasn't loveable.

A truth began to grow down deep in my soul beyond where a special light flourishes. God plants a faith seed in us. We feed and water the seed. It takes life in us, becoming like a plant unfurling and ready to break through the surface of the earth. Our faith

---
* John 17:24.

establishes itself in our living. Once God chooses someone, He does not change His mind.

Many people say that we have to accept Jesus for salvation. But perhaps He chose us first, nurtures a love for Him in us, and brings us through the world to keep us for Himself. Was His choice determined before we were born, before the earth was created? That moment of enlightenment planted a seed of understanding that has fed me throughout my life. I am convinced that I am not the driver of my life.

I couldn't run to talk to Mom about this notion, because then she'd know I had hidden my talks with God. Randy was too young, so I asked God instead. "Father, for a little while, can I climb into Your pocket and curl up to rest there?" I sometimes carried special things, like a rock or a toad, in my pocket.

"I welcome you to My pocket. You need not ask again. Whenever you have a desire, you can do so."

We both understood that He didn't have an actual pocket. The Father put His hand on my shoulder and I turned to look at Him.

"I love you because I chose to love you." He smiled.

"And I don't have to earn it?"

"No. It is not possible to earn My love. I chose to love you before you were born. It's a decision I made. It goes with you through your life. The creature cannot put the creator into debt.

"How do I get to heaven?" I asked while entering His pocket.

"The love I have for you draws you. Eventually, you'll realize the plan I have for you, and the substitution of the death and resurrection of Jesus who paid the price for your sin—it fully covers all of the price. Your entry to heaven is based on your belief that Jesus freed you from sin. You respond with gratitude. It is not something you can do on your own. I give you the faith to believe. That faith grows. You begin to see."

I was learning to communicate with God spiritually. I had learned earlier from Katy the intellectual basis of what He communicated, but it didn't reach the spiritual depth of what He said today. His pocket would always be a place to communicate, rest, pursue unfinished questions, and experience joy in Him. I had just gained a massive amount of new information in new ways, pushing my capacity to my limit. He understood this. Safe in His pocket, I could put the immense spiritual energy that swirled about me into a new space inside. It was a way to rest in Him, to be calm while that new space in me grew. My being in His pocket was a sign of trust, love, healing, peace, and utter dependence.

While my physical self sat on the large tree roots, my spirit self curled up in God's pocket. This allowed me to put the new pieces I'd discovered together and eased my return solely to the physical world.

Spiritual growth isn't easy, but calm came, and it was wonderful. His pocket became another sanctuary. It was a reversal from the church I knew. We put God in a sanctuary. God's pocket allowed a place for me in God. There I could absorb the new growth into the me I needed to be. Emerging from His pocket, I was revitalized, recovered, and strengthened.

I carried the book back through the cotton field, across the street, down the sidewalk, and into our house. I walked into my bedroom and laid the book carefully on my bed, front cover up. I walked into the kitchen and opened the top drawer, where I counted out four knives, forks, and spoons. From the second drawer, I pulled out four yellow napkins and set the table for dinner. Yellow napkins made the table look happy in a sunshiny way. My joy was rising like little, tiny pop bubbles. All was well in my world.

That night I began to read the Bible stories to Randy before we went to sleep.

To stay in God's presence and keep close, I used the Golden Bible and read to Randy the stories Katy had told me. It worked for me.

Love a Boll Weevil

This is a cotton boll. It contained soft cotton but was as rough as sandpaper.

The next day, I returned to the shade of the tree in the cotton field. It was so hot. Quietly, I began to hum "In the Garden."

> I come to the garden alone,
> While the dew is still on the roses,
> And the voice I hear falling on my ear
> The Son of God discloses.

Refrain:
> And He walks with me, and He talks with me,
> And He tells me I am His own;
> And the joy we share as we tarry there,
> None other has ever known.

> He speaks, and the sound of His voice
> Is so sweet the birds hush their singing,
> And the melody that He gave to me
> Within my heart is ringing.

> I'd stay in the garden with Him,
> Though the night around me be falling,
> But He bids me go; through the voice of woe
> His voice to me is calling.

I stumbled slowly through the cotton field among the rows of plants. I was still overwhelmed with yesterday's vision, but was able to think about it more closely. I stopped to stare at a boll weevil on a cotton boll.

Boll weevils are bizarre, a little like a praying mantis. I felt a kinship to the boll weevil. I, too, felt odd. I didn't mind being odd like those bugs if it meant being with God.

I looked closely at the bug. "Bug, I could choose to love you. You don't have to be special or loveable—just be a boll weevil. Life is simple that way. So, Boll, you just be you, and I choose to love you."

From that day, I loved a bug. I don't know whether I ever saw that specific boll weevil again, but if I saw one, it was mine to love.

I felt a need to study them. They were called evil weevils because of their destruction of cotton crops. I chose to love an evil weevil, but bugs didn't sin. They were doing the work of their species.

Boll weevils arrived in Alabama in 1915 and ruined the cotton crops by eating the plant with expeditious voracity. Their arrival brought destruction to crops all over the South that year.

To my amazement, in downtown Enterprise, Alabama, there is a monument to the boll weevil erected on December 11, 1919. The monument claims the boll weevil helped the area shift from one-product agriculture to a better economy of mixed crops and manufacturing. By being such a ruinous pest, this insect taught the town early on to set their feet on better economically sustainable footing. The boll weevil taught them to diversify.

One of the crops they chose to plant instead of cotton was peanuts. They also introduced further diversification with corn, peaches, and manufacturing. This area recognized how to see this bug.

I chose to love and learn the lesson the boll weevil had to teach. The unlovable are hard to love unless you look closely. You can sometimes see something unlovable meriting a statue in a town where there was once terrible destruction because it brought a huge benefit to those who could learn the lesson. Loving the boll weevil gave an Alabama town prosperity, while other areas of the South continued to fight the insects.

"Good job, Boll Weevil!"

It made me wonder whether any living thing was truly unlovable.

The town of Enterprise, Alabama, dedicated this statue to the boll weevil. People in Enterprise learned the lesson of the boll weevil and were blessed financially by listening to the lesson of the boll weevil. They taught me to love as close to the way God loves as I could understand.

After looking closely at the boll weevil, I wanted to be alone, to savor the new experience, to think on it, to look at the picture in the book again and again. At age six, I was filled with love for God that I now find astonishing. I learned love from God by loving boll weevils. My tiny love for God grew in my love for Him and in the boll weevil He made. My recall is still vivid more than seventy years later.

In years to come, the boll weevil parable came to apply to people as a whole. Both spent their lives in a rough, sandpapery environment. Boll weevils had little to give, only great need of a friend who wanted to take nothing from them—just be a friend. It was a way to follow in God's steps. My place was simply to follow what I saw Him do. Humans could learn from boll weevils. And I would follow God and love boll weevils to learn how to love people.

How would I know whether I was following God's steps?

I'd learn that people would literally tell me. A dear friend whose life was ending due to lung cancer sent me a tiny card. She was an artist and had made the card herself. I was surprised to see the card because she and I lived near each other and it came in the mail. I opened the card to read that since she had met me, she knows that God is alive.

I gulped. I fought tears. I held the card, gazing at the artwork, wondering what she'd seen in me that gave her that information. And then it dawned on me. She wasn't seeing me, but rather the One whom I follow—she was seeing Jesus in me. It was one of those "Let your light shine" moments. My light is Jesus Christ. Something I never thought about but learned from the boll weevil—my "follow God" experience learned in a cotton field in Louisiana.

It was from others that I'd know whether I walked as I should and moved on the path to become the me He intended me to be.

I stood from where I was watching the boll weevil. "Father, I love You."

He reassured me with a touch to my shoulder.

Never Poke Around

Animals that lived in our yard became pets. Toads loved the area under drippy faucets on the house.

An unforgettable experience taught me something in the winter of my thirteenth year. I had come home from school and sprinted off in my dress and sweater to the tree swing and the creek, and started swinging across the creek and back. As I tired of that, I jumped to the ground, the skirt of my dress flipping up on my back. I stood up quickly and shook my dress back to where it belonged. I picked up a twig and went down to the water's edge to see whether I could spot any little fish. I poked the stick into the ground mindlessly and then shoved it further down only to feel something odd in the sand. Something rubbery. I pulled the stick back quickly and with my hands dug down about a foot deep. From the sand, I brought forth a toad—a living toad—a big one.

Did someone bury a toad? Why was it underground? Clearly it was alive, but it seemed awfully sluggish. I washed it off in the creek. Then I understood.

I looked the toad in the face and said, "I'm so sorry. Please forgive me. I didn't know you hibernated." For someone who rarely cried, I made up for it with a massive release of tears while holding the toad by the ridges on its back so its legs dangled down as I looked into its eyes.

I needed to rebury the toad, but I wasn't sure if I reburied it, it would live. More tears began to fall.

"Oh, Lord, what have I done?"

I felt His touch on my shoulder. He was there.

"Lord, please let this toad have air to breathe as I rebury it. Let me not kill it. Please restore the toad."

Carefully, I cleared out the hole where I had found him. Gently, I returned the sandy soil to the hole over the toad, terrified I might smother the hibernating creature. I had been mindless. My mindlessness was like not seeing. I might have killed a toad through my thoughtlessness. That wasn't doing my job of seeing properly. Tears kept falling. I was burying a living toad, and I didn't know whether they constructed airways in the sand so they could breathe or what else might go wrong after I reburied him.

I did not pack the soil over the toad but gently smoothed the sand over the place. I didn't want animals to dig him up. I walked home, miserable.

Mom knew something had happened. "What's wrong?"

I burst into tears again. "I think I might have killed a toad."

She asked me to explain, listened carefully, then she said the toad was no doubt fine. Mom told me it wasn't my fault because I had no way to know a toad was under the ground. Neither of us had any idea that toads hibernated. She tried to comfort me. In some ways she did, but a large wound grew inside my heart. I never forgot that poor toad that I dug out of hibernation, washed off in the creek, and reburied. Sometimes I'd think of it and feel disheartened all over again. I had learned to see that mindlessly poking the earth with a stick might not be a good idea. I could not see through dirt. Something living might've been hurt, possibly killed by my mindlessness.

I considered my action that day as irrational and irresponsible. It hurt to realize how I strived to see and failed so miserably. Even today I sometimes feel a pang over that toad. Of one thing I am certain—I outlived it.

Part of the Body of Christ

I was baptized as an infant at Westminster Presbyterian Church in 1943. To me, public admission of belief is a visible step into church membership with the church meaning the Body of Christ on earth. My separation from this church of my youth happened at age five when we became military itinerants which caused me to see many things differently. My heavenly Father became sanctuary because He assumed the role to teach me when I no longer lived near Katy. Base chapels weren't designed foremost as cradle-to-grave developers of spiritual Christians.

Mom and Dad would do Bible studies with us from time-to-time or send us to the Base Chapel for Vacation Bible School or Sunday School. It was intermittent and focused on retelling the stories that were old to me.

As I saw it, God's pocket was another sanctuary. Rather than a specific part of a specific building, my sanctuary was anyplace where I was with God. I wanted to make my public admission of faith in the church body where I was baptized, the Westminster Presbyterian Church in Richmond, Virginia, among the people where so long ago I wanted to defend the Lord from the Yes/No noise.

In my mind, it was my home church. It was the place where I came to know God, though the church is no longer in the same building. The church refers to the people, not the physical building. That Yes/No vote resulted in selling that building and constructing a larger one farther west.

My special family in Richmond attended there. When in Richmond, I went there on Sundays. I wanted a godly-acknowledged entry into the Body of Christ, which, according to what I read in the Bible, was a single functioning body. I wanted to join the church where I felt familiar with my spiritual roots. A Base Chapel didn't have what I sought. I wanted to say to the world, I believe in and belong to Christ in a place where family and friends knew me. I might have had as many as thirty relatives and friends who attended Westminster at that time.

Katy put her energy and effort into my request and got approval to allow me to join the church at Westminster—with the proviso that I would have to answer questions the minister would ask me before the service so that he could approve my readiness.

In the early spring in1956, I made my public profession of faith at Westminster. I was twelve years old. I met the visiting minister to be approved. Katy told me his name was Dr. Richardson. As Katy talked to me about him, I could feel her awe of the man. I'd never seen her in awe of anyone. She cautioned me that he had a clubfoot and not to stare at his shoe which accommodated his disability.

Katy told me that Dr. Richardson had memorized the entire Bible and could start anywhere and keep reciting. Later I discovered that as a missionary to China, Dr. Richardson's memorizing the Bible was wise as a physical Bible might be confiscated and he couldn't do without a Bible. Carrying it in his memory made confiscation impossible.

Katy took me to meet Dr. Richardson in a room in the church building, introduced us, and then left us alone. I admit that as I sat down to meet with Dr. Richardson, I did notice his foot for a moment before I looked at his face.

I knew instantly God had planned for me to meet this man the second I looked at him. In a split second, I knew this man walked and likely talked with God. It was shattering in a wonderful way. As this type of meeting has occurred through my life, I came to call them "appointments." My appointments usually are for mutual learning. In this case, Dr. Richardson asked me questions and I answered fully and truthfully, and clearly to his approval. I could understand Katy's awe of him.

I shared with him my walk with God. He knew that I knew Jesus Christ and trusted in Christ for salvation. I shared the secretiveness of my time with God and why it was secret. I told him God had something for me to do for Him, but I did not know what. Now someone knew that I knew God. I considered Dr. Richardson a holy man. He didn't make fun of my view of the Body of Christ or why I wanted to join at Westminster. He simply listened to my answers to his questions. I wanted to cry for joy, but I held back my tears. When, shortly afterward, I was called up in front of the congregation to make my public affirmation of faith, I felt transported to the spiritual instead of remaining solely in the physical world. The Lord was there. He was pleased that I was doing this. I felt certain the congregation didn't see anything but the physical process, but there was so much more.

During the traditional ceremony, Dr. Richardson touched my shoulder, very much as the Lord would do when I talked with Him. A warmth passed from the minister's hand through my entire self. An unmistakable warmth transferred through him, and I changed. I could feel it. I was delighted. Then, the Lord impressed on me the verification that I was indeed changed in a spiritual way.

And then it passed, and I was back in the physical world, knowing that I had been transformed whether anyone recognized it or not. I'd had nothing to prepare me for that warmth or the transformation, it simply occurred.

I looked at Dr. Richardson's face and knew that I'd met what the Old Testament calls a righteous man. The honor of meeting one was special to me in a way I can't put into words. He became my model or prototype of a righteous man. I learned what was important in a godly way. He wasn't a flashy man whose name everyone knew and revered—far from it. He was a quiet, righteous man who clearly knew and loved the Lord.

When I went to find information for this book on him some fifty years after his death, only one person had any knowledge of him. That person sent me a newspaper clipping telling of his retirement with a photograph of him. Even the Seminary where he taught had no one I could find who even remembered he taught there, let alone anything about him. Oddly, I thought that was how it should be for a righteous man. It is right that people should remember what he taught about Christ, not the man himself. So much to be learned from this man!

I remember nothing from Dr. Richardson's sermon. I had been spiritually transformed by the Lord through Dr. Richardson and continued to relive the experience as the sermon progressed. I had not known this would happen. I was unprepared for the effects. The feeling was like nothing I'd ever experienced. It was like flying with angels, being in God's pocket, swimming in the glory of God, radiating joy in sureness of being part of the Body of Christ with something to do on earth for Him, and knowing He had a place ready for me when I died to this world. This was better than a feast in the presence of my enemies. Maybe it was all of those rolled into a moment in time. I didn't actually know if I had enemies.

God literally holds the universe together after having spoken it into being. This day's experience made me realize how entirely dependent I was on God for every aspect of life. At the same time, I could do things in my weakness because He empowered me to do things that were beyond my human ability alone. It was a duality that I was convinced came from becoming part of the Body of Christ, though in some ways, I'm sure it was there all along. It was as if I were empowered with nothing to do other than be prepared.

I felt the various ways of empowerment, trying them on spiritually, one by one, as if they were jackets. Each felt different. Through this experience I came to understand what would be treated as esteem or love whether for self or others. In my life, the question of my unworthiness never occurred. My esteem was targeted toward God, not myself. What love I had flew to Him—like the magnet to the refrigerator.

This spiritual step did not make me feel good or bad about myself, though spiritually I soared in love to God: Father, Son, and Holy Spirit. It did have an effect, though. I would come to treasure myself because He treasured me. I knew that His love would remain forever. I had been given a large portion of the single security that exists on earth—God's love. When esteem became an item to discuss, I realized I never needed self-esteem. I had God's love. I didn't need self-love!

Anole and Disbelief

An anole (a-no-lee) lived near where we lived on base in Savannah, Georgia. Once I saw one the size of a dachshund in the woods. The Lord was there. We didn't have phones back then that I could have used to photograph the animal.

We arrived at our new location in Savannah, Georgia, in the 1950s. What was then called Hunter Air Force Base was a Strategic Air Command facility during the Cold War. The delightful place is now called the Hunter Army Airfield. The Georgia landscape was a visible feast. Full of hardwoods and tropical plants sporting unimaginable color, all framed by Spanish moss dripping from trees. The views could capture your breath. Sometimes, morning sunshine broke into rays through the Spanish moss, and gently sang to my spiritual nature their songs in light rays filtered through the trees.

I was accustomed to spending time with God whether just being together or talking all the while enthralled by evergreen southern live oaks, yuccas, palm trees, oleanders, and azaleas. The greatest gift to me was the pine forest across from Traynor Avenue where we lived on base. The pine forest was reached by walking past our neighbor's side yard on an access path across a tiny creek where the far side banks were dome-shaped hills created by earth-moving dump loads of red clay earth. I thought of these mounds as the Red Hills.

The pine forest smelled clean with a brightness that delighted my senses. The floor of the forest was covered in needles, which had fallen over the years, in some places at least a foot deep. It was my escape from the skin-brutal sunshine while providing another spiritual retreat with God where we could speak aloud without being overheard.

I had learned in Savannah to drift to where my physical life met my spiritual, forming a good portal for entry into some places. I knew where they were. I'd ask for God's permission to enter though it wasn't necessary, and walk boldly through trees to be with Him.

Early on, I wanted to learn more about our wonderful pine forest. One hot summer day, I walked across the street and over to the tree where a rope hung down. A huge knot was tied at the bottom. I could swing on that rope across the creek and back or let go and drop to the ground beyond the creek.

Then came the Red Hills which I thought of as a barrier that I had to cross before I could enter into the forest and find my spiritual place to meet God.

The pine forest substituted as a type of church building for me, another sanctuary. The Lord would be there, not because He was tied to beautiful settings but because He was everywhere.

Sometimes I ran from one end of the Red Hills to the other, where, for a split second, I could feel a sense of weightlessness at the top, before descending to the valleys between the hills. To me it was another special place, I can see it clearly in memory, red clay and all, even today. And recall the pungent fragrance of the pines.

On that first day that I crossed the creek, I ran across the hills. Then I quietly walked into the forest where God welcomed me. In a sign of respect, I always made an effort to walk soundlessly on the fallen needles. This day, I walked farther back into the forest than I'd ever been. Deep in the forest, most of the trees were pine, but there were a few huge oaks that the lianas, called vines by the locals, would climb. Some boys would climb the lianas, or at least they said they did. I never saw them do it but they'd talk about it on the school bus.

On my way into the forest, I stopped. I smelled a snake. I didn't move. Then I saw an anole about ten feet away. Back then we called these lizards American chameleons, but most people call them anoles today. This was not a normal anole. It was the size of a dachshund. I was speechless. I wondered whether it was the source of the snake smell.

"You see that?" I asked in a whisper.

His touch on my shoulder affirmed that He did.

"Lord, I didn't know they got that big." Again, I whispered, keeping my eyes on the animal. This anole was brown and stood still on the brown pine needles. The anole had one of its eyes fixed on me or us or maybe just the Lord. I couldn't see the Lord, but could the anole? I didn't know.

"There is much you don't know," His quiet voice said.

It was not a put down, just a simple statement of fact. It was an assurance that I wasn't supposed to know everything. It was surety that all was well. It made me aware of the Lord's incomparable mind, and that with Him, I need not worry about anything at all.

"This is real? Not something You made for me to see that isn't real, like the steps to heaven?"

"Yes. This animal grew up in this forest. Remember this: there is much to see, and few see."

I was always excited to have new information. "I can't wait to share this."

"Don't be surprised if some don't believe you."

He sighed and put His hand on my shoulder. I couldn't see His hand, but I could feel the pressure. At that age, I didn't fully appreciate how it must have pained Him to know how often people failed to believe Him. Of all the people who've walked this earth, surely, He was the most unbelieved, and I was about to have the opportunity to experience not being believed in a miniscule way by comparison. An opportunity to share something He felt. What a gift!

In time, I let people know that anoles can grow as big as a dachshund, and no one ever believed me. Even all these decades later, no one has believed me.

One afternoon, late in the school year, the school bus bounced along delivering us to the Base gate. I had rested my head against the cool window glass for the boring ride home. The bus stopped, shoving us forward in our seats. I stood waiting until I could get into the aisle. I got off, stepping down the entry stairs uneasily as they were built for people with much longer legs than I had. I headed home, my arms filled with books.

"Hey, Bonnye!" Carl, the boy who lived at the cross street where we turned our bikes to head for the base pool, called out. "What's this I hear about a dachshund in the pines?"

I didn't reply.

"Oh, that's right! It was a chameleon!" The older boys with him laughed.

"Whatsa matter?" Leon, a grade ahead of me, shouted. "Got no more dog stories to tell? Cat got your tongue?"

They bent double sniggering and playing the fool. I stood still, watching them without expression. This was before cell phones. I didn't have a camera with me that day and I had no proof of meeting the anole.

Up to this point, I had naïvely believed that when a person spoke the truth, it followed that they would be believed. This unveiled the myth I'd taught myself. Without proof, truth tellers could easily be accused of lying. No one believed me when I shared the size of the anole. Then I remembered the words, "There is much to see, and few see."

I understood then, but that didn't assuage the discomfort, the prick of pain I felt being mocked and not believed again. Jesus must have felt that pain on the grandest possible scale. He had shared something He experienced as a human with me. I was in awe. That sharing meant a lot.

The boys seemed confused. Since they weren't getting a rise out of me, they were unsure what to do. Warren, who lived at the north end of the housing area, laid down his books and decided to see if he could get a rise out of me if he got physical.

Carl grabbed his shirt. "Leave her alone. She's not worth bothering with. She's also been taking judo on the base where she used to live in California for a couple of years. She and Jim were talking about it in the cafeteria." He said the word years with a touch of awe in a whisper. None of them took judo classes. I was confused. We only lived in California for six months.

Warren hesitated. He looked at the other boys. "You're probably right, Carl. Not worth bothering about," he said and whispered, "Took judo for two years?"

The boys left. It was clear they believed I could hurt them. And I wasn't about to disabuse them of the notion.

These thoughts of mine, thoughts of pain at not being believed, were as rocks in a tumbler through the years. The rough thoughts collided sufficiently with other thoughts, smoothing out the sides of the rocky thoughts and making the rough and sharp into shiny and smooth. But "Few see."

I wanted to be one who could see. As I fervently convinced myself I did, I had no idea what it was I sought or how hard it would be to achieve. I wanted to be a seer, not a surface observer.

A person with 20/20 vision can assume they see perfectly. That's what science tells us. But taking in something through the eyes is only a small part of seeing. Seeing what it is for what it is—is something else. As it was for Jesus, few people had any clue with whom they walked. Some made fun of Him. I "saw" I should not expect others to believe what I say when I speak truth, even if those others know me. I also "see" that I should consider others carefully. Will I stake my standing with God to hold what I believe about another person?

When people failed to believe Jesus, why should I expect anyone to believe me?

I also realized that I needed to learn to see and to prove, when I could. Furthermore, and maybe even more importantly, I needed to be slow to scoff at what others told me. I did not know with whom they walked. The Lord showing me the anole wasn't about the anole. It was this curious human thing of certainty in uncertainty. When we see, do we see? Do we question our assumptions based on what we see or hear? Do we do diligent research? I learned to be wary, to aim to see in truth what I saw, for I frequently erred; still do. I was no different from those who mistook Jesus as a weirdo or those who taunted me over the size of an anole. It is human to do so. Few see, including me.

Holy Eyes

It was afternoon on a hot day in Savannah, Georgia. I was stretched out on the grass at the edge of the forest in the shade. My Lord sat at rest nearby leaning against a live oak tree. With His back against the tree and some real distance between the houses and the tree, He would not likely be seen in the shade.

At twelve years old, I considered myself quite grown up. After all, I was the oldest child in the family. I watched clouds overhead during their afternoon drift out to sea. Life was good.

"I want to know You better," I said into the quiet of the afternoon. "I want to know how You see. You keep impressing me with the need to see, and I am just so slow to understand. I already know You see so much better than I do. Will You please show me what it is to see like You do?"

"Why do you want this?"

"I want to know You. I hardly know You at all. You know everything about me. I just know that the more I know about You, the more I want to know."

"You want to know even if it's painful?"

"I have no fear of pain when I am learning things I want to know."

"I will grant your request with a tiny amount of data. More could be disabling. Raise your hand if you feel too much pain."

I lay on the ground looking at the sky. I felt an unusual feeling, akin to nausea. I shut my eyes. When I opened them, I was unprepared for what I saw. There were all the data from what I thought to be creation to a future somewhere sometime. I think it had to do with weather. I could not grasp the data in time. By the time I could get an idea of a set of data, it was gone and replaced by something else. Some seemed to present in language and some in images, some of which were still and others moving. There was too much. Way too much! It went by too fast.

It was then I realized He doesn't see like we do. His sight was not limited in space. He could see in all directions with no blocking so that you could say He saw spherically. Time periods seemed to be in sync and out of sync chronologically. It was becoming painful to try to keep up with what was passing by. I raised my hand.

I felt as if my head would burst trying to follow these data one point at a time, but I found it impossible. The human brain cannot handle all knowledge related to a subject. At least this human brain couldn't. I failed on the first try. I should have seen how futile it was to try to see in this manner, but I kept trying. When I learn, and it becomes difficult, I don't give up, I try harder. I was overwhelmed and found it hard to raise my hand. I was exhausted. I had shut my eyes.

"Are you in pain?"

"Not exactly."

"Then what, exactly?" He knew what I would say before I said it, so I think He just wanted me to focus.

"You gave me limited data as You called them. You deal with all the data points involved with not just this earth but also for the universe. The depth and breadth of one of these is so great I can't follow a single line of sight, let alone multiples. And You have to deal with associated people and how they relate to the subject, values, needs, how the subject may be used, and endless issues. How many data points relate to earth?"

"The number is greater than the numbers you have. I do not need what I showed you. I know these things. I just gave you an example of the process of my vision, not the specifics.

It had never occurred to me that our numbering system was any less complex than any other numbering system or for that matter that other numbering systems might exist. All I knew about numbering systems was words, base 10, base 8, base 2.

I tried to pull myself up on one arm, but I had to give up and lie back down.

"Thank You for sharing that. My head hurts. But I have a tiny hint of the greatness of You, my God. You just showed me one single difference between us and it's so enormous, I had no clue how enormous it is. I feel that You've grown in greatness in exceptionally large strides, and truth is I've diminished to less than a little piece of sand. And that is wonderful! I want the biggest

God ever, and that is what I have. No other gods are gods! You are the God. Do You ever sleep?"

"I have no need to sleep."*

"We may be made in Your image, but we are so very, very different! I'd have to admit we're way inferior! I want my God to be so far above us that no one could argue with You—I only stand in shock at how phenomenally great You are. You stay in touch always in the maintenance of things but take the time to talk with people. You know when a sparrow falls. You are the God I want for always."

The Lord got up, came over, stooped down, and gently cradled my head in His hands and the pain left, though I was still disoriented. Yet, I had for a moment in time seen in ways that made me realize the extraordinary otherness of our God and the vastness of the Creator and what He had created. The distance and difference between us was now so huge that I couldn't begin to get my head around it and made me worship Him the more. This God was infinitely amazing. He gently pressed His thumbs against my eyelids and when I opened my eyes, my vision was back to normal.

"I gave you the maximum a human can endure without damage. I wanted you to see and it seems you saw much."

"I am just glad I know and love You, but even more so now. I'm so happy I don't have to be You. Those who'd want to be You, would, I think, as You put it—explode and cease to live."

He smiled. "Do you have any other questions?"

"When You know all the data, why do You write it down?"

"It's not written down anywhere, you saw into My vision process as if it were encoded into English."

"Do You ever tire of having to know all You know, all these details of being everywhere at all times—of being You?"

"Of being God?"

"Yes."

"No. I never tire."

"I'm glad."

He laughed.

---

* Psalm 121:3-4

MtDNA and Healing

These little pink cave fish are blind yet they know where they are and can find food in the darkest of darkness. I saw them first when I was in my teens. When I went back in July 2002, the cave had been amazingly excavated, but the fish were no more. People working there never knew fish once swam in the dark.

One day in 1958, a beautiful, clear sky arched over our area in Virginia. It was a Saturday, and Katy and I weren't at work. Katy and her friend, Susan Rivera, along with her son, Charles, and I took a day trip to the Luray Caverns to see a natural wonder. I was excited because I had never seen a cavern. Something else to see that the Lord had made. I wondered what I'd learn about Him.

Heading toward the cavern we passed a block from where Granny and Poppy lived. A familiar negatively inappropriate and conceit-filled thought crept into my mind. I loved my family, but from the day I was born, Granny, my dad's mother, was someone I wanted to avoid. I've been told that when she came to the hospital to see me, her first grandchild, I screamed my head off when she entered the room and only quieted when she left. I repeated that behavior any time she was near me for over a year. You just cannot teach a newborn baby complex human behavior, like being quiet even though the baby doesn't have any desire at all to be quiet. You cannot even teach that to an older baby, sometimes not even to an older child or adult.

As time passed, Granny and I came to tolerate each other. Granny was domineering, had strange ways with her children whom she also neglected and none of whom she ever told that she loved in a direct way. If asked, her response about love was, "I love all my children." She never focused on one child. She was a manipulator, expecting to be the center of attention. I didn't want to grow up to be like Granny. She was, I thought, a person to teach me what not to be, not a person to emulate.

I pushed down thoughts of Granny, reminding myself to live in the present. For some of the drive, I dozed, lulled by the sound of tires on pavement which made a noise from the seams in the road—not as loud as trains clacking at track abutments, but similar in sound and rhythm.

Susan slowed the car at the entrance to the cavern. I awakened ready for this new experience. We bought tickets and went inside. At that time, there wasn't much to see. What I remember vividly, however, was the small waterway with blind pink fish at the end of our short walk. The fish were a little longer than my hand. Despite their blindness, they had areas where eyes would have been. I figured those eye things were vestigial at this point. I had heard of blind cave fish, but I'd never seen one.

The stalactites above us were oddly shaped. It was an unexcavated cave, so there was little to see. It was startling, however, to see such forms that grew from drips over long periods of time. We were led to a narrow path with a handrail on the left side. The stairs were the exit to the cave. We'd probably spent only fifteen minutes in the cave.

"Hold the handrail. I'm gonna turn off the light for one minute," the tour guide drawled. "You'll probably experience dark like you've never known. Don't be scared. It'll only last one minute. Anybody here too scared to hold on for a minute? Let me know now, and you'll have time to go back to the entrance."

Nobody left.

"Okay, I'm gonna turn off the light."

The cave was total blackness. This, I thought, was how it was just before Jesus spoke light into existence. The darkness was virtually tangible. No one moved. It was deadly silent. The fish, a level in the cave below us, I was certain, knew exactly where they were. They needed no eyes to find food or each other. They lived in that dark blackness for more hours than the lights were turned on, and before that they never were illuminated.

The light came back on. It was a short walk to the exit.

On the way to find something to eat, we stopped at an overlook on the mountain drive. I followed a path and kneeled down on the grass and was instantly with the Lord.

"It is time to turn loose your concerns about your Granny."

"Lord, she is my ancestor. I don't want to be like her."

"People in general do not understand fully yet, but you are from the line of women in your history, not the men. There is a new scientific study which will be available soon. Your Granny is of your father's line, not your mother's. She is not a linked part of you. I have a plan for everyone. My plan for you has no relationship whatsoever to your Granny. It relates to your mother, your grandmother, your great-grandmother, and so on, all the way back on the female line. You are closer in heritage both physically and spiritually to Katharine than to any other person in your family. You may substitute her for your grandmother. The genetic and spiritual plan is there."

I noticed He had used Katy's Christian name. Of course, He knew my grandmother, Mom's mother, who had died before I was born.

Essentially before MtDNA was common scientific knowledge, He explained the concept so that I understood the genetic answer that solved my long-standing dilemma. My Father's explanation removed a heavy burden. A burden I wanted to be rid of, but I didn't know how. As always, He did. In that moment, I soared spiritually with a large bird in the sky.

Unbeknownst to me, Charles had walked down the stone pathway to where the physical part of me kneeled. What he saw, I assume, was my soul looking over the valley below. I was startled to end my flight as I realized I was not alone. I was horrified. No one that I knew had ever seen me when my spiritual state was heightened way above my soul. People are physical with a non-physical soul. The non-physical soul is personality, intellect, and so on. People also have spirits, a non-physical part that can interact with spiritual beings and things both good and evil.

"Did you see the eagle?"

"That's not an eagle." He laughed. "That's a turkey buzzard."

"What's a turkey buzzard?"

"It's a kind of vulture." He offered his hand to help me up. "It's time to go." We walked up to the car.

To my great relief, he did not ask what I was doing down there. He must have seen nothing unusual.

In a simplistic way as we drove home, the Lord provided more information for me.

It didn't make the issues with Granny go away, but it made me realize I was not of her genetically in the sense that I was of my matrilineal line. That helped me let go of the negative emotions I had about her. It's not that I now believed my negative emotions were appropriate. They weren't and I knew that. But they had been with me since birth, and getting rid of them was beneficial. When Granny went into one of her manipulating spins, I could reassure myself that I was not "of" her, and the sting of horror from our past encounters would never touch me ever again.

What I realized while in the cavern was that Jesus, before He spoke light into existence, experienced a dark that was hard for us to imagine. The darkness in the cave with the light extinguished was almost palpable; the lack of sound added disorientation to the sense of mental uncertainty in the silent darkness. But Jesus must have experienced the sensory orientation of the blind pink fish. He would have known where He was despite the absence of the help that light and sound provide—another way of His "seeing" that we don't experience.

Lion of Judah

The Chain Fountain at Maymont Park in Richmond, Virginia, is a lovely addition to the landscape. A lion encased in stone is at the top of the steps.

One summer when I worked in Richmond, Virginia, I had a free weekend. Susan Rivera's son, Charles, and I planned a picnic for Saturday at Maymont Park in Richmond. Charles wanted to show me the waterfall near the Chain Fountain. I had never visited either place. I loved my work as a proofreader, but all week I looked forward with delight to a weekend adventure outside.

From the air, the gray stone Chain Fountain seemed a reasonable choice to visit. It was Charles's suggestion. I'd never been there. Essentially, the Chain Fountain was three sets of double parentheses, one above the other, with circles positioned between the parentheses. The parentheses looked like broken chain links. At the top, a stone wall stretched the width of the fountain surround and a lion's head protruded from the wall supplying water from its mouth.

Charles carried the picnic basket, and I carried the blanket as we descended the steps to the fountain where I came to an abrupt halt.

The air was different. It was alive with the electrical feeling of the Lord's presence. I was fast leaving the physical. The head on the stone lion silently moved ever so slightly. For a stone of that size to move, it should have made a terrible sound. It didn't make any noise at all.

"Give me the blanket," Charles said. "I'll get us set up."

I had forgotten Charles. He took the blanket and disappeared.

The Lion stepped from the fountain's wall. It stood huge, strong muscled, and amazing. It increased in size. "I am the Lion of Judah," it said in the quiet voice I already knew as the Lord's.

The Lion of Judah is the one who can open the sealed book at the end of times. Pre-Christian, it means the messiah. To me it was Jesus. I was transfixed, lost in the Spirit, wondering why He would appear to me this way.

"You have work to do for Me." His voice resonated, so I assumed the rest of the world could hear. My chest was like a guitar box responding to strumming the wire strings. He shook his mane.

"What do You want me to do?" I asked.

"It's not yet time."

Anger filled me. "Then, why are You telling me this now?"

The Lion looked down on me with an air of disdain. It circled at the top of the fountain, looked at me again, decreased its size, and stepped back into the wall without another word.

I slumped. Jesus appeared as a Lion, and I'd offended Him. But I didn't understand what the offense was, unless it was my anger, except my anger was more than enough. Shame flooded me. I stood there a while, wondering whether He'd return. He didn't.

I left the fountain and followed the path I'd seen Charles use. He had set our picnic up by a lovely waterfall.

"There you are," Charles called to me. "I wondered what you were doing."

"Just looking at the fountain." I spoke to him in the physical world with residuals of the spiritual world still attached to me.

How could I share with him what had just happened and how torn I was between anger and shame? He would have thought me crazy.

I was utterly broken inside. I was supposed to be enjoying a beautiful Saturday in an exquisitely lovely spot, but our easy chit chat from earlier had changed due to my moodiness, an attitude I almost never experienced. An invisible four-foot-thick rock wall had fallen between us. We couldn't talk through it. We said short words back and forth, both aware that something had happened. Something that I was unable to explain.

I was ripped apart. There was something missing. The Lord had not imparted all He came to say due to my anger. Or was that what I had to learn? Govern my anger or I would miss what I needed to know? Was that the day's lesson?

The electric feeling to the air had vanished.

* * *

From that day to this day in my old age, I remember the event at the fountain in exquisite detail. I remember almost nothing of the picnic except arriving at the spot and that it was a lovely place.

What I do remember is that from that moment I began to question whether I was even fit to be a part of a couple. I had a whole different life that I shielded from others. I would never depart from my spiritual life, for despite my anger that day, I treasured it above all else.

My considerations drifted to the future. If I were ever to marry, my focus would be God, not a husband. That would definitely be unfair. From that moment, I understood that my life, though shared with some, was most probably to be lived alone. I have to admit I was not bothered at the life-changing thought. It affected all I did from that time.

I would become God's worker. I knew with sharp clarity where my heart lay, if I gained no other enlightenment that day.

Preparing to Prepare for Work

After my summer working in Virginia, Mom and Dad sat me down for a conversation. I was fifteen. I thought we'd already had that talk, but this was different. Dad began. "We thought we should talk, because there is something you must do, and you have to plan now."

Mom looked at her hands for a moment and then at me, "Because you're a girl, your life will be different from your brothers. Things will be harder for you than for them. They can get good jobs without a college degree. You can't."

This was unexpected. I knew for years about the talk, but not this talk.

Dad said, "In high school, I want you to avoid typing classes. Take chemistry and physics."

I was shocked. I had never considered a typing class, but Dad's comment came out of the blue.

"If you can't type, nobody will suggest you'd make a good secretary for some man. You should be where the man is, needing a secretary of your own. You may at some point need to support yourself. You may need to work just to make ends meet. You may just want to work. You'd lose your mind in a routine job where you had to follow the lead of someone you didn't respect—someone who reasoned poorly or was uncreative in problem solving. You need to have work, whatever it is, that requires you to think hard, to solve problems, to consider novel solutions, and to contribute."

"Don't get us wrong," Mom said. "There is nothing wrong with being a secretary. I've been a secretary. But I worked as a secretary to bring in a little extra money and because I wanted to work. Our livelihood depended on your dad's paycheck, not mine. The truth is that women are viewed as expendable in the workplace. Katy, for example, is head of the Proof Room at her work. Women work for her. Their work requires detailed precision. Katy would never be considered as head of the Press Room. Only men work there.

Their work is valued far greater than the women's work. Yet, if the Proof Room let a lot of errors go by, they'd lose business. When men in the Press Room make errors, proofreaders find the errors so they can be fixed. Both are valuable to the company, but they are paid differently."

"That's not fair," I sputtered.

"Life's not fair," Dad interjected with a tone of cold reason.

I looked out from the window.

"There is much to see. Few see." I remembered the Lord's saying.

"Lord," I spoke silently. "I don't want to see unfairness. I have an extra burden that the boys don't? Why should I? Here in the South, chivalry insists men help women with their burdens, not add to them. It's inconsistent. To me, it makes no sense at all. Intellectually, I'd have to jam it together for it holds paradoxical thoughts."

"In time, you will see. Your vision will clear. Strange motivations tie this together." He pressed His hand on my shoulder and then was gone. I was pretty sure neither Mom nor Dad knew the Lord had been there. Mom and Dad certainly gave no indication of having heard Him.

From that moment on, I focused my near future on obtaining a college degree. I began to see it as a key that women required in order to open doors that were already open to men.

No typing classes. I took chemistry and physics. I was fascinated with chemistry and found the math easy. Physics did not interest me. I could have used typing when it came to doing papers for college though.

While working that last summer after having graduated from High School, I applied to Mary Washington College in Virginia, close to family that stayed in one place, unlike Dad, who moved around the United States because of his job. I was excited about the upcoming college interview for admission.

Mom, Dad, and my brothers drove up from Georgia for a summer visit and they drove me to Fredericksburg since I likely wouldn't be returning to Savannah. My interview was scheduled with the Dean of Admissions, Michael Houston. I liked him. He had the demeanor of a military officer, and I had been around those most of my life. I felt at home. As we talked, the issue of tuition arose, and I told him that the cost of education would be tough.

He eyed me seriously. "After graduation, are you willing to teach?"

I assured him that I'd love to do that.

He leaned back. "Then, I have good news for you!"

"What's that?"

"I'll see that you have a full scholarship for the four years it'll take you to get your degree."

I sat there for what felt like an eternity with an open mouth before I could form words again. "Are you sure?"

"I don't make such statements lightly. You can count on it. You will just need to teach in-state for four years."

"I'm delighted. Tuition paid and assurance of a job!" I was ready to dance on the ceiling. "Thank you, thank you!" I wanted to hug him but I comported myself as much as an adult as I could manage. In Virginia at that time, girls were taught to act like ladies. I never felt I fit in. I liked it about as much as I liked wearing dresses.

The interview ended soon afterward, and I practically ran to the car to tell my folks the good news. I could hardly contain myself.

College Days

I finished writing my answers on a Shakespeare exam of twenty-one plays. I had studied long and hard. The blank I was to fill in was the name of a character in the "Merchant of Venice." The name that escaped me was Shylock. Everybody knows Shylock. All I could remember is Shelley's poem, "Ode to a Skylark." He calls the skylark a blithe spirit. I kept thinking of a blithe spirit having run off with my memory.

That fall, I became a student at Mary Washington, living in a dorm and struggling with the imposed "lady rules" which were many and confusing. Actually, they were called rules for women, but my distaste for the Virginia practice of having girls go through a type of finishing school so that they'd be socially acceptable translated in my mind to "lady training" which slopped over to rules and I put these down as "lady rules."

One day, my roommate came flying into one of the meeting centers on campus carrying my raincoat. I was outside at a table in the sunshine enjoying a conversation with the Dean of Women who happened to be at the same place at the same time. I was shocked to be interrupted.

"It's after three o'clock and you're still wearing Bermuda shorts!" my roommate said carefully when she recognized the Dean. "If you put this on, you'll be safe."

She left as abruptly as she'd arrived. I was astonished. If it was somehow wrong to wear Bermuda shorts after three, how did putting a raincoat over the shorts change anything? Just because you hide something doesn't make it right. In my mind, that made it worse. I did not understand these deportment concepts at all. I saw nothing right or wrong in wearing Bermuda shorts. And as to how time of day got involved, I had no clue.

"How is it, Lord, that I can look at the same thing as other people and yet see so differently?"

"Your eyes are designed to see only a part of what you are looking at. Your eyes move and additional parts are filled in by your brain. What isn't seen by your eyes may just be filled in through logic. Your environment and your training both affect the weight of importance you place on what your eyes perceive.

No wonder people have such trouble seeing, I thought.

A similar thing happened another time my roommate arrived back at the dorm.

"I bet you have no idea what happened today," she said, enticingly.

"What?"

"Do you remember skipping down the sidewalk and then running up the library steps and back down like you ran in a V?"

"Yes. What was remarkable about that?"

"Dean Houston was behind you on the sidewalk. He skipped on the sidewalk just like you did. He followed you up the steps and down and then he went one way and you another."

"You're kidding." I was amused.

"No, I'm not. Most people on campus are deathly afraid of him."

"For what reason? He's a very nice man," I said with a little force.

"He's so gruff."

"You mean the military manner? I'm used to that."

"Well, seeing him do that sure surprised me!"

"I wish I'd known." I'd have grinned and asked how he was doing on that fine day.

At the end of my first semester at Mary Washington, I made an appointment to see Dean Houston. I was ushered into his office where he invited me to sit down.

"What brings you here, Bonnye?"

"I am not a good fit here. The lady rules are driving me crazy. I'd be better off at Richmond Professional Institute." RPI was viewed as the "hippie school."

Michael Houston was quiet for a moment, a look of amusement on his face. "I wish I could say that I'm surprised. I'll be sorry to see you go, but I do understand. By the way, I have some more good news for you."

"What's that?"

"I'll see to it that your scholarship follows you to RPI. You can count on it to get you through school if you still want to teach."

"Oh, yes."

"Then I'll see to it."

I thanked him and we shook hands. He wished me well and I left, ready for the next adventure in my education. Had the Lord been in human form, I'd have run to hug Him, thanking Him for touching hearts for my benefit. Mr. Houston was a blessing to me.

My transfer from Mary Washington to RPI went smoothly. RPI was great for me. RPI had moved from a social services school located in repurposed houses to a well-known arts/drama college with a focus on social professions in 1917. A couple of years after my graduation, it merged with the Medical College of Virginia to become Virginia Commonwealth University.

At RPI, you could attend class in jeans or shorts, and even flip-flops if you chose, and focus solely on studies without a required dress code or other behavioral or time-of-day rules. The school was in rapid transformation. Where Mary Washington was the establishment, RPI was evolution before the eyes, alive, growing—on the wild side— the hippie school, inside a very conservative, gentry-oriented city. I was not a hippie, but I loved the evolution of the school and being part of it not to mention the freedoms it afforded.

The summer gave me time to create a plan for my education. I was going to RPI to purchase the key that would give me entrance to a professional job with my future work teaching. It fulfilled a promise I had made to my parents.

I entered my second semester with no idea what I could teach. I took the general required courses, but I thought long and hard about what to specialize in. I thought of my SAT scores and my path became clear. I did well in the humanities, but I skyrocketed to the moon in math and science. I'd choose an education to round myself out, and I would aim to teach English. I put myself in that direction and never deviated. I had a plan. I even liked grammar.

I'd sit in my tiny room in my great-aunt Katy and great-grandmother Neenee's apartment, and considered the ironic choice I'd made to teach. I didn't really care for school. Give me a forest and the Lord and I'd soak up spiritual matters like a sponge. Give me access to something like the Richard's Topical Encyclopedia or Britannica, and I was delighted intellectually. I went to classes because it was required. But school was just a means to an end for me. I would give it a modicum of effort, but I wasn't planning to ace every course. I wanted to learn what I wanted to learn, and simultaneously wholeheartedly pursue a degree, the key to professional opportunities.

My journey had taken me to RPI and I'd agreed to teach. I did not want my classes to do unto others as classes often did unto me—teach little that I'd need for the future in a boring way. I did enjoy term papers as I could learn on my own and synthesize my results into a coherent point of view. Term papers usually took me a day to write. From the first day of class, upon hearing that term papers were required, I'd start making mental notes of areas of interest, and then think of a question to ask. The term paper would answer the question. After mulling over the subject boundaries of the term paper, I'd hone that down to something I could examine.

Back then, students used a card catalog in the library for identifying relevant data. We lacked the extensive reach of information available online to students today through computers and, as if by magic, phones! Maybe it's just as well. I'd have lost all my social skills if I'd had access to the internet back then.

The day I'd write my paper, I'd arrive at the library when it opened, carrying an unused spiral-bound notebook, sharpened pencils, and note cards. I'd spend an enormous amount of time at the card catalog, looking for books on my subject, and cover a table with all the books I picked out. It wasn't necessary to read the whole book, just focus on the relevant data.

I'd bookmark the pages I needed with three by five cards. As soon as I'd gathered my data, I'd concentrate. In a process I have never understood, I'd relax, and the data would come together in my brain to create an organized whole.

Once that overview emerged, I'd start writing. If I wanted to quote someone, the books were in front of me. I knew which book contained the quote and the card marked the spot. By the end of the day, I'd have my paper written in the notebook and references jotted down on note cards that I could put in order. All I needed to do was to return home and type up the paper.

The only problem I had was with classes where the professor required an outline of the paper. I found outlining awkward and time-consuming. When I tried it, I'd deviate to such an extent from the outline, that outlining time was wasted. To create the required outline, I had to write my term paper and then outline it. The positive part here was that I always was on time with term papers, especially those requiring outlines. As a future educator, I found the idea that all brains worked the same an absurd concept. Not all people needed to outline. My brain did that while I stared off into space, often with a cup of coffee.

There were two courses I adored. Speech for Teachers was taught by Raymond Hodges, the head of the Drama Department. We learned the international phonetic alphabet, how to project our voices, and how to relax the throat so as not to go hoarse. We also learned what I considered the most critical and valued element for teachers—how to modulate the voice. I really liked Professor Hodges. How I wished I'd had that course before my first day as a copyholder at the printing company where I had my first job.

The second course that held my interest was a high-level course in my senior year about Shakespeare. The professor, E. Allen Brown, was head of the English Department. We covered twenty-one plays in one semester. He knew his subject inside and out. It was killer, but it was also an incredible challenge. I loved the challenge. I worked harder at that course than any other. A friend of mine and I studied before the final exam for two full days. Before the exam, I knew the title of each of the twenty-one plays that contained a character named Bartholomew. That's how intensely we studied.

The day of the exam, I went to the far back of the room to avoid distractions. The final was multiple choice and fill-ins. No essay responses were required. I ripped through the material speedily and then sat and sat and sat. One line to be filled in remained. One character's name was supposed to be written on there. I knew the character; I knew every bit of what he did. But I could not recall his name.

The play was Merchant of Venice. All I could call to mind was "To a Skylark," a poem by Percy Bysshe Shelley, who called the Skylark a "blithe spirit." I imagined a skylark spirit the size of a human, stalking me in the back of the room—blithely. Momentarily entertaining, but a definite distraction that didn't help. But for that line, I finished the test in fifteen minutes. I had to sit there trying to recall the name for the remainder of the hour. I'd shift position and hold my head in my hands. Nothing helped relieve my squirming.

Out of curiosity, Professor Brown walked to the back of the room where I was. "Is anything wrong?"

I wrote in the margin on the page to avoid disturbing others. Pointing to the empty line, I wrote, "I know this guy. I know everything he was involved in. I cannot remember his name! All I can bring to mind is Shelley's 'To a Skylark.'"

The professor burst out laughing in an unchecked, seemingly uncharacteristic guffaw. It startled the other students, not to mention me. Looking directly into my eyes, he said, "Relax, you'll find it." He returned to the front, still chuckling.

Just before the end of the hour, I recalled the name—Shylock.

I took my paper to his desk. He raised a finger to stop me, flipping through the pages to see what I'd written.

"I knew you'd get it. Skylark—Shylock, far away but so close."

"S _ yl _ _ k and S _ yl _ _ k"

The letters made a perfect connection for a sight reader. I discovered some of my deficits in college. I didn't hear or discriminate sounds well. For example, I now live near the city of Anchorage. If you listen to locals talk, often they leave out the "or" or just the "o" in the word Anchorage. It comes out Ank-ridge or Anka-ridge. It's local. Something I rarely notice anymore. It didn't cause me difficulty when I heard it the first time. But at RPI a word hit me that drove me crazy—menoretidation.

It occurred in the adolescent psych class required in my BS program for English-Education. For three days, the professor lectured while I sat there taking notes wondering what in the world he was talking about.

I asked a classmate, Ellen, "What is he talking about? I've been hearing menoretidation over and over and I don't know what it is. I cannot find it in the dictionary or make sense of it from context."

She chuckled. "Say it out loud three times."

I did. Nothing. I shrugged.

"It's two words—in Southern."

I was still in the dark.

"It's mental retardation."

At that point I was convinced I had a problem. Ellen and I did have some laughs over that. From time to time, she'd ask how my menoretidation was coming along.

One day, Dr. Brown passed me in the hall. He was my advisor, and he had asked us to bring our Graduate Record Exam (GRE) scores to him. GREs are comparable for graduate programs as the SATs were for undergraduate work. Because the English-Education program was new, Dr. Brown asked us to take the GRE and share our scores, because he wanted to see how the English-Education students were doing. I'd purposely been avoiding stopping by his office, as my GRE scores really bothered me.

"Bonnye," he called out, "I haven't seen your GREs yet. Do you have a moment to stop by my office?"

I nodded, not wanting to stop, but knowing it was unavoidable.

"I have the score data in my purse." I sat and pulled out the envelope, handing it over to him.

"Well, these look great."

"Not to me," I said, probably petulantly.

"Why so?"

"I chose to teach English, because it was my weak area; science and math were my strong points back when I took the SATs. In college I wanted to round myself out. My GREs look like my SATs, so I didn't succeed in rounding myself out."

He chuckled and observed that I was different because most people pursued their strengths. He also assured me that I had rounded myself out. I had an excellent grasp of English. He was delighted with my GREs.

While at RPI, I spent a lot of time at home in the afternoon talking to Neenee. I adored her. Neenee was born in 1880. One weekend Katy drove us all over the Church Hill area in Richmond. That's where Neenee lived in her youth. I'd ask her about how everyone managed things before some of our modern conveniences were available. She'd share tidbits of life that had changed so much.

One day I was home working on a skirt made of pale green wool. I did crewel embroidery around the bottom and up the front. She had the television on watching her two soap operas. An announcement came that President Kennedy had been shot.

We looked at each other. It was more than our minds could handle. That kind of thing just didn't happen in the United States. I wanted to pray for the Lord to save his life but that would be a futile prayer, I somehow knew he was dead.

For days, we went about our daily routines conscious of the huge impact of our President's death. We were numbed.

I finished the skirt and wore it a few times. Eventually I gave it to the Salvation Army. Emotion had attached to the green skirt, and I wasn't comfortable with the reminder.

My time at RPI went fast. Mom and Dad threw a reception for me at a hotel following graduation. We had snacks, cake, and punch. I felt tremendously honored, and the party was so adult. Mom and Dad gave me three hundred dollars as a down payment on the car I wanted to buy. At that time, three hundred dollars was a lot of money, the equivalent of over three thousand dollars a quarter way into the twenty-first century. I was overwhelmed with gratitude. It was a stunning car, a 1965 burgundy Mustang fastback with white leather seats and black carpeting. It drove like a dream, or so I thought.

I had an interview at Chesterfield County where Susan Rivera worked. She was Supervisor of Guidance and Counseling, and a longtime friend of the family. My interview with W. W. Gordon, Superintendent of Schools, went well. I assured Mr. Gordon I'd like to teach at Thompson Middle School or Huguenot High School. Both were a comfortable commute from my home in Richmond.

Susan and Katy laughed for years about my making it clear which schools I preferred. They assured me most interviewees would have been pleased to get any school. But I didn't expect Mr.

Gordon to be a mind reader. He wouldn't know my preferences unless I told him. I had lived a military life. My view was that if I wanted something, I'd ask for it specifically. If no, I hadn't lost anything at all. I might get my preference. In my case, it worked and I was contracted for Thompson.

I bought my car as soon as I received my teaching contract for teaching eighth and ninth grades. The school was a great match. I quickly learned that if I could capture the imagination of middle school kids, they'd knock themselves out to please. They also could spot anything fake from a mile away. I appreciated them tremendously.

The Unforgivable Sin

Before the school year began, I stood in the backyard and looked at the sky. I could see many threads moving around as if placed into position on a loom with other threads woven over and under, back and forth across them. Sometimes the colors changed. I made myself become still and focused.

I had read Walt Whitman's "Song of Myself," but I didn't exactly like that poem, for it disturbed me. Now I had a revelation: I was proud of having my degree and a job teaching, I did celebrate myself, but I had not done those things at all. Although I didn't like Whitman's poem, I realized why now. I didn't perceive it to be true, and I was allowing myself to believe the lie it contained.

I sat down cross-legged by the little tree. How could I have been so blind? "There is much to see. Few see." When the Lord shared that with me, He certainly knew my weak area.

"Yes, Lord. I was blind to this for a long time. You even told me 'There is much to see. Few see,' and I didn't see."

I had subconsciously credited myself with what the Lord had done. It's clear in Matthew 12:13-36 and Mark 3:29 that ascribing to Satan what the Holy Spirit has done is an unforgiveable sin. I saw ascribing to self or anyone else what God had done sin as well.

Pharisees said that the miracles done by Jesus, such as casting out demons, were actually done by Satan. How could I have been so blind and arrogant—blind to an amazing extent?

The Lord had touched the hearts of one person after another to bring me to this point—having a degree and a teaching job. It was as if the Grand Weaver had led my parents to lay the warp on the loom in our talk about my need for a degree, woven strips of weft by touching Dean Houston to finance my education, touching Dr. Hodges and Dr. Brown to provide me tools and understanding of teaching, adding more weft from Neenee and Katy who taught me how to be me, slipping Susan Rivera into the weft because she knew Mr. Gordon who interviewed me for my first teaching job.

Susan also helped in my student teaching days by providing transportation so I could get to my student teaching location. Mr. Gordon did indeed interview me and contract me to teach at Thompson. The Lord, even long before had created me so my SATs reflected what they did as He guided me to teach what I had credited myself for choosing. I'd need these skills much later in life.

God planned the weave and designed the woven tapestry of my life to that point and would continue to do so for the rest of my life. Who was I to accept what He'd done as my handiwork? Ascribing His work in bringing many things together to place me in this position at this moment as my work—that was blindness and sin.

I knew in as much crystal clarity as I had ever known that I am not the master of my fate, I am not the captain of my soul. Truth was I was carried on the shoulders of others in almost all I did.

That poetry quote, with the nots removed, is from the poem "Invictus" by William Ernest Henley. As with Whitman's poem, "Song of Myself," I disagreed with the view of the author.

God taught me differently—I belong to the Lord; I am His. I see when He opens my eyes. I aim to follow His desire.

I was so overcome with emotion that I could barely get to my feet and walk back into the apartment. An incomparable lesson. He was reforming me spiritually in seconds, a lesson I'd never forget. I would purpose not to fall victim to such pride again. With permission, I climbed into His pocket to rest until, again, my spiritual body could accommodate what I'd just learned. The transformation I had at age twelve was reawakened. I would fight for Him, even if it meant fighting myself.

Someday, He'd have a job for me. He'd told me that when I was age six. I felt a huge need to be prepared. And then, I understood. Of course, He would prepare me. My spiritual life was a puzzle. I found little pieces and didn't arrive at the whole lesson until I put the puzzle pieces together years later. And even at that, I had to guard myself with the truth: He was the weaver of my life, not I. He guided me to find puzzle pieces when I didn't just see them straight off. Pride must be dealt with. It was a poignant realization. Not so hard to say, "I have a pride problem." Harder and a better learning experience to say, "I almost committed the unforgiveable sin."

Teaching

To my delight, teaching and I were a fantastic match. Over the years I taught at Thompson in Chesterfield County and Richmond City after they annexed our part of Chesterfield. I sponsored the school literary magazine, pulled the students together to put on "Midsummer Night's Dream," headed the foreign language department. Thanks to the principal's deciding that I would also teach French since I was certified to teach it. Nobody gives you a list of what you're certified to teach, so it was a surprise to me. One year I taught a class of physical education due to teacher shortfall. I never even minded the amount of work I had to do on my own time at home.

In January, during the second semester of my first year teaching, my great-grandmother Neenee died. She was in the hospital for a brief time. I'd been attached to her since I was born, and her loss tore me to pieces. She'd been telling me her end was near so I could be strong for Katharine—her name for my great-aunt Katy—but I refused to believe she was near death. I adored Neenee and had lived with her off and on since I was born. Her's was the first death I ever experienced of anyone I loved deeply. The event made me loathe hospitals, as if they were the cause of her passing.

I tried to reason with myself that it wasn't true, but I carry a horror of hospitals to this day. I tried for about a month to interact with others and could do it at school, but with others who knew Neenee, it was hard. Others who knew Neenee might want to talk, and talking was the last thing I wanted to do. I was grieving. I'd wake up at night hearing her voice, as if she called to me. I could hear her voice as I drove back and forth to school. Time made her absence easier to bear, but it was still devastating. Richmond was having fierce snows, and she was the last person buried at Oakwood Cemetery before it closed down due to the hazards of the heavy snow. School had been cancelled, for which I was grateful.

I spent a lot of time in the Lord's pocket during those days.

At the end of my first year of teaching, Susan Rivera brought me an offer from the School District. They wanted me to go to the University of Virginia in Charlottesville to get my Masters. They'd take care of all expenses. They wanted me to become the head of the English Curriculum for the District.

I thought about it, but I had to decline. I loved teaching, but I wasn't crazy about taking classes. If I did what they wanted, I feared that I'd be out of the classroom and working from a tiny office somewhere. I don't think Susan was happy with my response, but she claimed to understand. I tried to explain that I had three more years to teach to fulfill my contract, but she assured me that could be waived. I didn't accept the offer. I wanted to teach.

The second year of teaching, I was drafted to teach French, head the Foreign Language Department, and teach English Grammar and Literature classes; I had many issues to deal with. I had not been taught French the way the new textbooks taught it which was by memorizing conversations. I had been taught grammar in both conversational and literary forms in depth. When a student of the language, I was expected to speak the language rather than repeat memorized sentences.

As a teacher, I improvised. The students I taught would learn French grammar and how to put words together to create their own conversations. I did try to make it fun. For French lessons, classes often got a page with six or more cartoon sequences of frogs where they had to write their own dialogue.

At the time, I didn't know the connection with frogs and the French. My cartoons were something I knew how to draw, not a political statement. At Christmas, we sang Christmas Carols in French. The students also learned songs in French from printouts of the lyrics and a record player.

A former student dropped by after class one day. She wanted to tell me that the French teacher over at the high school had mentioned that she could always identify my students, because not only could they converse, they also understood French grammar. I appreciated the compliment and thanked her for sharing.

In my second year of teaching, I also started the school's literary magazine which published student writing. I continued that for the remainder of my time there.

The third year, I pulled the students together to put on a production of "Midsummer Night's Dream." I had them make some changes to re-write the dialog into the language of the day. I wanted sexual references and jokes removed or anything else that was not appropriate for school. They did a fantastic job. After they read their lines in class, I was amazed at what they produced. During the project, one of the students in the play developed a brain tumor. It was a fast-growing cancer, but Pat made it through the process and was part of the final production. Her success pleased me as much as anything else we did.

The donkey head for Bottom was made from papier mâché by the Art Department. It was a true to nature representation of a donkey head, and was done well enough that when on the actor's head, it didn't interfere with the audience's ability to hear his words. I called my college to see whether Dr. Brown would like to attend. To my utter dismay, I learned he'd had a stroke and wouldn't be able to join us. For someone as intelligent as he to be struck down by a stroke was a source of great sadness to me. I was not accustomed to sadness.

Knowing that our school would have children bussed from inner-city communities next year, I spent the summer before my last year of teaching creating a new grammar approach and I prepared to teach in a different way. I took a class through the College of William and Mary on *Bloom's Taxonomy of Educational Objectives*. It caused me to see things differently. That study taught me to see with greater purpose, just as the Lord had taught me that there was much to see and few see. I learned how to organize materials to give learning a deeper dimension by generating a real interest in the subject and causing social interaction among the students to bring the black and white students together faster.

That fall, I had classes with students registering IQs from sixty-five to one hundred and fifty. I had never found much meaningful data from IQ scores. All I figured is that it might mean that there were differences in the group. I knew first and foremost the students needed to talk to each other, and it was my role to help them break the ice.

On the first day in my English classes, I put the students into integrated groups of three or four. Then I explained that they were to create a slide show. I explained that they'd be using the rubber-based ink images from magazines and contact paper to make slides for the overhead projector. They had to agree on a single word and find music that they all liked. There were no records at school, but all groups found music at home quickly. Then they had to check with each group to be sure there were no duplicate words. The slide show was required to include images that helped to define the word. I gave them instructions how to make the transparencies, then stood back and watched.

The students were exceptionally nice to each other, if a bit shy. A few days into the project, excitement developed and they were talking to each other. As the days passed and they were close to finishing their projects, the principal, Bill Caraway, knocked on my door.

"Can you get them to quiet down?" he asked me. His office was directly across from my classroom.

I stood as tall as possible reaching my full five-foot-two inches, and replied, "No! They are interacting with each other and working together. I won't tone this down for anything. Come in and watch."

"I can't right now." He retreated back to his office.

After the students finished their projects, I invited teachers whose planning periods coincided with my English classes to come and see the show the children had put together. A few came and those who came liked what they saw.

The students' shows featured words like friendship, love, and hope. The only music I remember was the instrumental piece by Mason Williams, "Classical Gas."

During that time, concerns of the children's differences were overcome by working together on a goal and producing something pleasing—even more than just pleasing. Doing a good job of meeting the goal became primary to everything else. They practiced on the overhead projector to lay out the slides they'd made on the screen, until it was almost seamless to the beat of the music.

I was so touched by their work together that I teared up watching them run through their shows. In each case, they chose exceptional visuals to define their chosen words and put them on the overhead projector to the beat of the music. I was so proud of them.

My introduction to grammar lessons was first to impress on the students how critical it was. Knowing good grammar and not knowing could easily make the difference between two candidates for a job. Learning grammar could open doors in their futures. I tried to make it clear that I genuinely cared about each of them and wanted the best for each individual.

I set up a self-instruction course based on *Bloom's Taxonomy* with one objective per sheet. The students learned the lesson and checked their work using answer sheets I made available on a bookcase in their classroom.

Rather than write on the sheets, I requested that they use a sheet of paper or a notebook. At the end of a series of sheets, I placed a red star. That meant a test.

I said "First take a lesson sheet and learn it yourself. When you check your answers, if you missed some, you need to repeat the learning sheet. If you have trouble, ask someone who's further along than you are to explain it. Someone who understands it. If you can't find help, come to me. When you reach the star, that means it is test time. If you want a little extra time to study, take it. When you are confident you know the material, tell me and you will sit at my desk to take the test. I'll give you the answer guide when you finish the test. You can check your work to know whether you made any errors. It must be completed while you're in class. Then, I'll show you your line in my grade book and you can record your grade."

Entire classes would sit in surprise when I laid out how they were to learn grammar. It was a method I'd learned at RPI, and it worked very well with my students.

I'll never forget how hard they worked to learn grammar. At the end of class, one of my students stopped at my desk. "Miz Matthews, can I share something?"

"Please."

"Today, I knew the answer and helped a White girl."

"I am so proud of you! Find a way to celebrate." I extended my hand, and we shook.

His grin grew wide. We were making the first year of bussing in the South into something genuine. It filled my heart with warmth. The children were way ahead of the adults.

As he left the room, I smiled at the Lord whom I knew was there. What an absolute treat for that student to have had such success! At that time and in that place, his joy was well earned, for it was a milestone. I'll never forget that moment.

Another Black student stopped at my desk one afternoon. "Miz Matthews, can I touch your hair?" She was normally shy, so her question surprised me. At the time, I had long, dark-blond sun-streaked hair. Her curiosity about my hair touched me.

"Of course."

She reached out and touched my hair. She ran her fingers through it. I grinned to match her grin.

"May I touch your hair?"

"Yes." She leaned toward me.

"Oh," I said, "I love the way your hair feels." It was so soft.

She smiled, but it faded fast. "Miz Matthews, when I go home, and it gets dark, I hear guns shooting in my neighborhood sometimes. Do you care?"

"Oh, honey, of course I care. Please, please be careful. I'll pray for your safety."

"You will? You'll pray for my safety?"

"Certainly. I want you to have a long, wonderful life."

"Thank you." She left my room with a tiny wave.

Midway through the first semester, it occurred to me that no one ever tried to cheat. I had only on the rarest occasions run into cheaters in prior years because it was frowned on by other students. There might have been one or two each prior year. All of this year's students really wanted to learn. They were actually excited to learn how to diagram a compound-complex sentence. From my point of view, I'd never seen such eagerness to learn grammar. I had reached my goal: to foster an eagerness to learn. I'd have loved to have learned that way myself.

I had for quite some time been convinced that IQ tests were measuring something but not necessarily how well students would do in school or life. What I found was that on a grammar exam at the college level (the way I designed the exam), every single student from my classes made nothing less than a C. That includes students with low IQ scores from the 1960s.

Becoming Mom

I opened my eyes. Shut them. Reopened them. It was definitely morning. A Saturday. "Lord," I called out quietly. "Thank You for this day. I dreamed last night. I dreamed I'd adopted a child, a daughter. She was about two years old. She had on a smocked pink dress tied with a sash in back. She had blue eyes and blond hair. Are You telling me something?"

"I know you want to have children. I also know you have no interest in marrying. There is a way."

"You mean I can adopt without being married?"

"If you want to adopt, write a letter to a state adoption agency and tell them what you'd like to do." He added directly to me, "I'll lead you in this effort."

I contacted the Children's Home Society of Virginia to see whether there were children that could be adopted by a single parent. To my great joy, they decided to use me as a test case for single parent adoption. I filled out all the paperwork, had a home study, and waited.

He'd led me. I had a phone call that summer.

"Hi, Bonnye! It's Jenna Jones. I'm calling to see if you can help out this summer. We have an awkward situation. Can you handle a disabled child on a temporary basis? We have a child that needs to be moved from where she is. It would not count against you if you don't want to adopt her. We just need to move her as soon as possible. Since you are off for the summer, it occurred to us you might be able to help us out."

"I'll be honest, Jenna, I hadn't considered adopting a disabled child. It's not something where I have any experience or knowledge. If the child needs a move to where she'll be safe and cared for, yes, I can do that. My personal dream is to share my life with a child who can fully share in summer trips and learning a wide variety of things."

"The birth mother was a child herself. Her parents made her wear girdles to conceal her pregnancy. It affected the child she carried. I'm trying to keep the little one from being institutionalized. If you can help on a temporary basis, it would definitely solve the problem."

"I'll do it." I wondered whether I was doing the right thing. But I realized it was just for the summer and the child was in need.

As summer was ending, Jenna called. They had a place for the special child. It was time.

"Lord, is it Your desire to have me adopt this child?" I asked.

"What did they ask of you?"

"To take her on a temporary basis."

"You did that?"

"Yes."

"So what do you not understand?"

"I guess I'm just trying to get Your view of what I should do."

"You have done it already. She has found a good home for this child. Do not be anxious. What color hair does this child have?"

"Dark brown."

"Does that not answer your question?"

"Oh. I hadn't thought of that." My dream had shown a child with blond hair. I wondered when I returned to teach whether I'd see that little blond-haired, blue-eyed child in the dream.

The Lord knows all things. In the first part of December during my last teaching year, Bill Caraway, the principal, came to my room and tapped lightly on my door. "You have a phone call in the office."

"Now?" I asked stupidly.

"I'll be back in a bit," I said to the class.

It was Jenna Jones. "Do you still want to proceed?"

"Absolutely."

"The day you get out of school for the Christmas holidays, you can pick her up. She's four and a half months old. Please be here before four-thirty."

I finally got the words out. "I am so excited."

"Good! I'll see you then."

Mr. Caraway stood nearby looking at me. He'd been leaning on his door frame watching me.

I spoke to him. "The day we get out for Christmas, I get to pick up my baby. She's four and a half months old." I smiled from ear to ear. I definitely had motherly desires. "The Children's Home Society decided to use me as a single parent test case."

His mouth dropped open and his eyes widened. "You're adopting a baby?"

"Yes. And I'm really excited. I can't have one on my own or you guys would fire me, but I can adopt." I bounced back to class.

Completely awed, I went to pick up my daughter. I decided to name her Katharine and called her Kate.

When I arrived at the Children's Home Society and saw her, reality hit. My daughter was so little. I gently reached down and picked her up. I was overwhelmed. She was beautiful. Her eyes looked into mine with openness. My life was about to change. So was hers. We had to make it a good change.

Would I be a good mother? Too late to wonder now. Over Christmas, I took her to visit relatives. She was a good baby and was happy meeting others. We had all of Christmas break to become acquainted. We did go out but spent most of our time at home, just getting used to each other. Life was good.

Kate was a good baby, and my maternal nature blossomed. Whenever I looked at her, I wondered how it was that the Lord had me dream of her as a toddler.

Before the second semester began, I was alarmed to learn that Mom had what they thought was intestinal cancer. Mom and Dad had finally settled in Seattle, where Dad worked in retirement at Boeing as an instructor pilot. For the first time ever, my family had developed roots. Katy would come to visit us every other summer.

My concern over Mom was genuine and I wanted to be there. I called Jenna Jones to discuss moving to Seattle. She reassured me that they would support the move and that, when it was time to take the legal steps to formalize the adoption, we could do that at a distance.

Susan helped me untangle the process to leave school mid-year. I had already completed the years of teaching required by my scholarship. Movers loaded my few possessions. Kate and I flew from Richmond to Seattle to start a new life.

When I got settled, Katy and Susan contacted me to let me know that my teaching replacement was in the newspaper taking credit for creating the grammar program I developed over the prior summer. I wondered what she was doing with my students now. I had taught the grammar semester, and the new semester was time for Literature. Katy and Susan were outraged. They thought I should contact the newspaper to ask for a correction. I thought about it but decided if the new teacher had such a need for praise that she'd claim someone else's work as hers, I'd not interfere.

I asked the Lord to forgive her.

Heavy, Heavy, Heavy Air

The air was heavy, heavier than I'd ever felt. I was home alone. Something was off. I was living downstairs in Mom's house in the Seattle area, having moved there a few years earlier. My daughter was at a birthday party. It was quiet in the house. I used the basement level where there were two bedrooms, a kitchen/living room, full bath, and an enormous all-purpose room. The bottom parts of windows let light in but the view was sparing on visual elements.

I went to the door and opened it and stepped on the concrete steps that led up to the side yard. I noticed there was a small growth of mold around the drain on the bottom level of the steps. I noted that for memory and climbed the steps to the edge of the stairwell. I sat on the edge looking at the gray sky and the incredibly lush green grass at this autumn time. I never had lived anywhere that autumn grass was any color other than some shade of brown. I still hadn't become accustomed to green grass in the fall. I'd have loved to have walked barefooted on the grass, but I wouldn't. I'd get slug slime on my bare feet. It's hard, I discovered, to remove from skin.

The heaviness remained. Odd, I thought, and then I became more attentive. "Lord," I asked, "You there?"

"Of course."

"The air seems odd—terribly heavy today. Is there something off in the weather?"

"Not at all. You'd be more likely to find your answer by searching inward."

"Thank You."

We returned inside and I went to make some coffee. I love the distinctive scent of it. While the coffee was completing its process, I put a few logs on the holder in the fireplace over some partially burned ones. I lit a paper wad and slid it under a few light pieces of wood. The coffeepot clicked. I went over and lifted the pot from its heat source and poured my cup full. Fragrance initiated salivation.

I sat on the sofa and put my feet on the small pillow that was on the coffee table. Looking at the ceiling, I realized that was not the source of the heavy air. My thoughts returned to John 3:16, a verse I'd known since early childhood, one Katy had me memorize. "For God so loved the world, that He gave His only Son that whoever believes in Him should not perish but have eternal life."

I had been ruminating over this verse for about a week. I understood it. It was easy. I understood it even when I was very young. But something disturbed me about it. People said the verse identified the requirement for salvation. Once you believed Jesus's death on the cross was the price of salvation from the wages of sin and that He was our sacrifice for our entrance to eternal life, we had the gospel in miniature. We simply needed to be grateful.

I felt something missing. But what? So Jesus "bought me out from hell." Suddenly a big shiver ran over my skin.

I had lived in the southeast United States. People bought people there for a time in our history. Some cities marked places where concrete blocks on the street documented where slaves had been sold to landowners mainly to plant, tend, and harvest cotton for great plantations all the way down to little farms. Slavery was become a national disgrace—a super sensitive subject. Some slave owners saw slaves as less than human and treated them poorly.

Surely, Christ didn't buy us for slaves. Or did He? Is that what I was missing? And it would follow—if bought for His slave, have I responded as His slave in any way or just ignored the whole idea?

Coffee forgotten, I stared into the fireplace. My thoughts flew in the face of typical Christian teaching that we have freedom of choice in what to believe, not that Christ was buying us for slaves. Yet something felt familiar to me. The air lightened up a bit.

The freedom of choice issue barely touched me. I believed as reformed Presbyterians do. I understood the doctrine of predestination; God's irresistible grace described as holy rape of the soul was not a foreign concept to me. Is this what was causing heavy air to surround me? Or was my little mind off on a wild goose chase? I focused on the flames in the fireplace as if on pause.

I went through the steps in the story of the crucifixion of Jesus. This time it was as if I were there up close watching every step along the way. I was aware of the horror of it all. It hurt in a strange way. Some big tears slid down my cheeks. The heavy air was back, pushing me down. The cost of my salvation was so high, too high.

I breathed out the word, "Lord."

"Lord, I took my sins so lightly. I wasn't worth what You had to go through. But I'm eternally glad You did it. How can I be both happy and pained over the same thing?"

Reality was crushing me. My coffee was cold on the coffee table. I was doubled up in pain that hurt as if it were real. The fuller vision of what Jesus had to experience to buy me out of hell was too much to ask, but sacrifice had rules, and this is why He came to earth. The sacrifice had to be blemish free. No human is without blemish and so could not make the sacrifice. Christ is the only one who could make a sacrifice acceptable to God. God-man. He was both in order to fulfill His mission.

He sat beside me.

"Sit up. It's done. You must move forward. Accept that you have been forgiven."

"Did You buy me with Your sacrifice to be Your slave?"

"Think on it. We will talk of this in the future. There are things I would have you do. Consider that."

What We're Designed For?

As my Father asked, I'd spent a lot of time wondering whether I was His slave and whether it was appropriate for Him to ask me to do things.

My brother, Randy, brought the term slave to our Bible study, knowing I'd been troubled over thoughts I had about this. He introduced John MacArthur's book, *Slave*. I studied the term slave and discovered that it was likely my relationship with God had given me the desire to follow Him. Was He leading me, training me? It seemed to me that He was as I examined it at a distance.

A church could explain spiritual progression to members. When I was kid after I moved to Louisiana, I didn't have that opportunity because I no longer went to church often. Add to that asking parents was out of the question. I needed a place where I could get more information about God.

My study taught me a lot as I reviewed my life. There was a verse, John 3:16, that makes a person think if you had checked that box, your salvation was assured. I knew that verse from studies with Katy before we left for Louisiana. I thought that was all that was required of us Christians. But something about it bothered me. I was left with a feeling that something was missing. I was convinced from that unresolved earlier memory work and later stumbling over the passage that John 3:16 was not an end-all but maybe a beginning.

Recognition of one's need for Jesus is only the earliest of beginnings. Words from Jesus's brother James floated up from my memory: "Faith without works is dead."* As Randy talked about his findings with his study of a possible follow up to John 3:16 in our lives, my earlier feeling that the verse was incomplete somehow took on life again. That was only the beginning and from there a place to grow was infinite. The only fitting time for it to be considered an end-all would be for those in the thief-on-the-cross position, one whose life is about to end. The thief-on-the-cross

---

* James 2:26

recognized and believed Jesus had the power to save him. He asked for it, received it, and then he died. Think how many people have called that thief to mind to teach about salvation. For someone at the edge of death you're trying to reach, that thief can demonstrate that it's never too late for John 3:16 alone to provide salvation. For the new believer, for example, it gives assurance that it's never too late no matter his age.

So John 3:16 gets us into belief. Then, belief with gratitude grows love in us. That love urges us to be useful to God, not as a broken slave but rather as one who would gladly be part of the Body of Christ for God's work on earth. That's what I sought. I believed John 3:16 to be the beginning for us, belief. Then belief became works from love.

I went to the door when I saw Randy's car drive up. Mom was in pretty bad health and on Sundays Randy came down from north of Seattle where he lived to participate in Bible study with us. The three of us really studied and since we were few, sometimes this went on for hours and hours until we were satisfied with soul food. Then, we'd eat food for the physical body.

That Sunday, Randy arrived with a new term: doulos, a word from MacArthur's book, *Slave*. Doulos is a Greek word for slave. It can also be used as bondservant or servant, but the tendency is to see that particular word as slave, since other words can indicate the unpurchased one who does work for another for wages. I was shocked.

And then from MacArthur's book these words struck me: "True Christianity is not about adding Jesus to my life. Instead, it is about devoting myself completely to Him—submitting wholly to His will and seeking to please Him above all else. It demands dying to self and following the Master, no matter the cost. In other words, to be a Christian is to be Christ's slave."* It's not about me; it's about Him.

Instantly, I was reliving my downstairs doubled-over-in-pain experience of several weeks ago as I was overwhelmed by the thought of the last hours Jesus hung on the cross before He died, taking my sins on Himself as a sacrifice for me so I would be justified for the eternal sanctified life in God's heaven.

---

* Taken from *Slave*, page 22, by John MacArthur. Copyright 2010 by John MacArthur. Used by permission of HarperCollins Christian Publishing. www.harpercollinschrisrian.com.

And I asked my Father, "Did Your Son buy me for a slave?" Wow! Quick answer, thanks to Randy and the book he shared, we were bought with a price, an extraordinarily heavy and acceptable price, the perfect sacrifice of Jesus.

I listened to Randy explain what he understood, and I'd also continue to study. I had the certainty that doulos had meaning, seriously significant meaning I had to grasp. I took it as having meaning to us as slave with the sense that it took over what was expected of the Christian after John 3:16's—believing on Him. I committed to becoming a slave of Christ's for the rest of my life. As James 2:17 puts it, "Even so, faith, if it hath not works, is dead." If you love someone but fail to demonstrate it, then your love is without meaning.

My heart leaped when I realized doulos was slave. I welcomed being a slave to Jesus Christ. He is wonderful, caring, thoughtful, filled with love. He knows a love we barely grasp the edges of. He did not purchase us for His enrichment, but rather out of love for us. He doesn't need us. He reaches to us in love for our enlightenment.

For once I saw in the way God had been urging me to see. I saw the thing itself and its significance. It was a type of Jesus's saying to the disciples, "Follow me." There it was. I wanted to follow Him. In very small ways, that's what I had been doing since I was three years old. Had He said, "Follow me," when I was three?

I thought of "In a great House, there are not only vessels of gold and of silver, but also of wood and of earth; and some to honor, and some to dishonor. If a man therefore purge himself from these, he shall be a vessel unto honor, sanctified, and meet for the master's use, and prepared unto every good work."*

I lifted my words in the holy name of Jesus to the Father in prayer: "Father, let me be to You a vessel unto honor, sanctified for Your use. Call me a slave or a vessel; it doesn't matter—just let me follow You. When You give me a task as part of the Body of Christ, make it effective for the glory of Christ. Keep me on the path and out of the weeds. Have me walk in the spirit to be always prepared and ready for Your use."†

---

* II Timothy 2:20-21.
† Galatians 5:16-26

Dad Sees Angels

When Dad saw an angel, I was shocked. He was one of the most analytical people I ever knew.

One evening when he was in Argentina, Dad finished flying the line with his students who were in the last part of their training as pilots in 1970. They went to a bar to celebrate. Someone in the bar poisoned Dad's drink. It turned out that the culprit assumed Dad was tied to World War II German war crimes. It was twenty-five years after the European victory. Dad definitely looked to be of German heritage.

Following the war, many Germans fearing retaliation had fled to South America and Argentina was a frequent destination for them. There were some religious groups that followed those who fled in order to extract revenge from the Germans. Emotions remained high there for long after the war's end.

Some Argentinians apparently considered killing Dad was quicker than trying to find out if he actually was a war criminal. What a thought!

The attack wasn't personal. He just looked the part. Dad didn't die, but following the poisoning he experienced cognitive problems that sluggishly worsened over time. Even though he couldn't fly planes safely afterwards, Boeing kept Dad employed as long as remotely possible. He had some skills that Boeing valued including his ability to draw. He reached a point eventually where he could stand in the kitchen with a glass of milk and literally sleep without spilling it. He'd wake up and continue mid-sentence with what he was saying when he went to sleep.

As time progressed, he'd roam around the house at night. In one of his night-time waking trips, he wanted ice cream. He got up and ate some. He also dropped the container on the floor and left it there. In the morning, Mom skated across the kitchen floor on the melted remains of most of the half-gallon. After this, I moved back in to help Mom.

The poisoning event caused many changes in Dad. One day, my daughter was playing in the yard as I took time to admire the plants. Dad looked surprised when he glanced at me.

He walked over, looked beyond me with eyes wide and said, "Do you know you have a group of angels around you? Really big angels."

It was the last thing I'd ever expected to hear Dad say for he was extremely analytic, but I was delighted he could see them. Frankly, I was unaware of the presence of the angels until he pointed them out. I checked. They were there.

I grinned and assured him I saw them, too. Maybe he could see the angels because the poisoning he'd experienced had taken off some of civilization's, society's, and the military's blinders that he'd had to wear in his adult life. As a pilot, for example, he'd seen UFOs, but had to act as if he'd never seen any rather than risking being accused of having a psychosis. Maybe God just cleared his vision in the yard, and with me, he had the freedom to say what he saw.

Shortly after that, Dad moved into a nursing home. He realized that my mom was suffering from lack of sleep and he wanted to make life easier for her. Doctors believed he had Alzheimer's, though his autopsy later proved that he didn't. The move to the nursing home and medical misdiagnosis, however, enabled him to go to the research program at American Lake in Tacoma, Washington, where he could help contribute to research. That was his goal at that point.

The chaplain there reported to Mom that even he had had spiritual help from Dad. Dad was blessed at the end of his life that he could still give spiritually to others.

Before he died, Dad received confirmation that indeed there had been an attempt on his life in Argentina.

Flashlight

I decided to ride the bus to work in downtown Seattle instead of driving. I had replaced the car but also bought an annual bus pass. That gave me two hours a day to read books without interruption.

One day, I'd gotten off work at the Federal Building at four-thirty and the wait for the bus was longer than usual. There had been snow earlier, and it continued to fall. The depth had reached about four to five inches. I was happy to have brought my moon boots to work with me.

The bus was an hour late and then there was an hour to ride home. With moon boots and my fur coat, warm hat, and gloves, the cold wasn't bad except on my face. In a plastic bag, I carried my work shoes and book. I also had a purse in the bag. Even though I wasn't carrying much, I was grateful when the bus finally arrived.

I enjoyed the ride while I read. Arriving at my bus stop, I stepped off the bus, and began the mile walk home. I loved my moon boots. Even though they looked funny, they added a wonderful spring to my step with a deep foam bottom inside and they gripped the ice, their bottoms made of actual tires. The walk was dark with only a few street lights. Snow clouds were thick. Flakes fell quickly. The snow was silent, magical.

About halfway into the walk, I complained. "Lord, it's really dark here. I'm having trouble seeing where to put my feet."

To my utter shock, light appeared instantly where my feet would step. Stupidly, I looked up and verified what I already knew—there was no streetlight in the area. I skipped a few steps despite the moon boots and my fatigue, laughing. I spun in circles, arms flying out to the side. I loved what the Lord could do.

"Thank You, Father. That is so much better." I twirled. "Please, will You make it shine a little farther ahead of me?"

"No."

"Why?" I stopped walking and stood still. It was time for me to be serious. I didn't want to miss anything.

"I gave you a gift. You will be able to see ahead, so you are prepared for what comes in your life. You do not need far vision. Just a little ahead will suffice for you and your work."

He wasn't talking about seeing in the dark, I realized. He was telling me He'd prepare me for what was to come in my life. "Father," I wondered, "is the time right finally for me to do the work I have to do for You?"

He answered the question I hadn't asked aloud with the weight of His hand on my shoulder and the words, "It nears."

"Wonderful!"

Snow continued falling, and the Lord's flashlight shined bright, brighter than any flashlight I'd ever had—illuminating six or seven feet ahead of me. No beam from above, just light where I needed it. Nothing superfluous or garish. Just meeting the need; no more, no less.

Explode?

My daughter, dear adopted daughter, had been asleep for an hour or two. On my return with a cup of coffee, I took a moment to peek in at her resting peacefully. What a heartwarming sight. I returned to sit at the table in my bedroom. I had been relentlessly pursuing the Lord that evening, knowing that I would find Him. I had learned so much, and that made me realize how little I knew. I wanted more and more, and was never satisfied. He taught me that some things personal to me are not for me to reveal to anyone else. What I can share, I share. I pressed Him hard for more that night. This comes closer to the line of separation of shareable and not shareable. What cannot be shared is omitted.

When I asked for more from Him that evening, He surprised me. "If I provided any more to you now—the amount you want—you'd explode."

"Explode?" It was one of those answers that made my head spin.

My mind raced and I sat with my head resting on the backs of my hands. I knew He was telling me something I'd have to spend time studying. There would be no easy answer this evening.

I thought back to the stairs to heaven vision which I had at the bayou when I was six. After that vision, I had felt so huge. The same thing had happened when I learned about God's pocket. I had to decompress until my spirit returned to its original size. I felt a huge need to decompress after those events—to return to my own size. Sometimes my learning from Him caused me to feel my spirit literally expand beyond my real size. Is that what He meant? There was a limit on how far I could expand? I actually expand?

During another session with Him, I asked, "Lord, You told me earlier that if You provided more information to me at that time, I'd explode—will You please help me understand?"

"I meant exactly what I said. You'd burst from too much internal pressure. It would be lethal. You are not configured to take in what you requested. When you live in heaven later, you will not be limited by your present design."

"Thank You, Lord. I'll think on that."

A previous experience with Him rose up in my mind. He'd permitted me an extremely brief vision of what I called "holy eyes." When He spoke of seeing, He meant literal seeing and also understanding—a combination of both. He didn't split them into two parts.

For a split second, I had seen in all directions with far better than eagle-sharp vision. I understood things in incredible depth. What I saw provided complete data that I knew instantly in multiples. I've tried to explain by saying it was as if an extreme super computer tied to vision and cognitive processes were implanted in my mind and I knew the totality of the contents in that computer all at once. It was an enormous shock, and I didn't have the capacity to remember details other than the context of the experience.

Now, He gave me that experience as a learning tool. It was as if what He showed me was the size of a grain of sand not as compared to the sands on earth but in the universe that His utterly otherness encompasses. My grain of sand was tiny, yet for me it was too large to understand.

As always, I was slow to grasp the full meaning of explode, but I learned something that night. In human form, I'm not configured to take in at one time all I may want to learn. The Lord teaches me what I need to learn, not what I may want to learn. He teaches me in the quantity I can take in.

I think what He teaches me is not factual knowledge, such as we learn through schooling, but rather is wisdom which comes only from Him. Individuals may have different capacities for different things.

Crazy or True

This is a beautiful unfurling fern leaf, what we call a fiddlehead where I live. Some people fry them and some restaurants serve them while they are curled. I ate them once at the Space Needle in Seattle.

John called out. "Hey, Bonnye, you gotta see this. Come over here. Quick!"

I heard such comments fairly often when I worked at the United States Civil Service Commission in downtown Seattle in the 1970s. People there knew I delighted in seeing rainbows or beautiful, unique sights that frequented our view from the 26th floor of the Federal Building.

I'd follow the caller to see a great round rainbow overlying the buildings uphill from us on the opposite side of the building from Elliott Bay. Another time someone called me to come to see a rectangular rainbow laid out between the Federal Building and Elliott Bay. I had seen round and rectangular rainbows from planes, but never from a building. It was a significant diversion from work. Another time someone called me to see a rainbow moving out over Alki Beach and Elliott Bay. Someone even called me over to see a fascinating plant.

The head of the Training Department stood beside me, apparently watching the rainbow also. He was a psychology major and for some odd reason, he was curious about what made me tick. Without moving his gaze from the rainbow, he muttered, "It takes nothing to make you happy."

"A rainbow is a beautiful, natural thing with a spiritual connection. It brings me great joy to be able to observe it. I prefer that to physical things any time," I replied. "Sometimes, when I see beautiful things like this seemingly out of nowhere, I find solutions to problems. Things will fall apart. The earth may be damaged as we would see it, but it will be here long after we're gone. To be part of it is a great privilege. Beautiful things also give perspective."

I came here to this fantastic view to think when I had a project or was plotting how to write something. When I was stressed, I looked out there and said to myself, will [whatever is stressing me] matter one whit a thousand years from now? The answer was always negative. Shoot! It won't even look like that a thousand years from now. I turned loose of whatever the stressor was, and I went on, unstressed. I realized then my stressors could have no lasting power.

"That's your answer to being happy all the time?"

"No. I'm happy all the time because I know God loves me."

"How do you know?"

"I walk with Him. He tells me."

That last comment put a halt to the questions. Truth sometimes does that. As a psychologist, he knew I was of sound mind. I did good work. I was without question a happy person. Everyone knew that. Walking with God was a totally foreign element to him. A foreign element that explained a lot.

To make a comment like that either meant I was a total crazy crackpot or was actually telling the truth. One or the other. Take your pick.

Someone called him, so he smiled and went to deal with it.

Quicksand at the Toutle River

I might have lost my life to quicksand at the Toutle River into which melted glaciers from the Mt. St. Helens volcano flowed following the eruption of 1980. My brother, Randy, caught me just as my leg dropped to mid-thigh in an invisible rushing mass of water and silt. We raced with our children to high land. Signs had not yet been posted regarding quicksand hazards.

Randy and I were curious after the eruption of Mt. St. Helens to see the damage that had been done. Oh, we'd seen the video from television programs, but that never provides the reality of such a monstrous scene. As soon as the initial viewpoint across from the mountain was set up for public viewing, we took his son, Mom, and my daughter to see the destruction.

What remained of the mountain was jaw-dropping. We saw some half-buried vehicles, only too aware that humans, some no longer alive to walk this land, had been connected to some of those vehicles. Being there made the two dimensional television images of the eruption real in the three dimensional world. The giant, old-growth trees, downed beyond numbering, were aligned unidirectionally on the horizontal. The size of the trees took my breath. The trees. They made something inside me break. Animals were hidden, if any survived at all, but birds brought life and sound to the scene. I wondered whether they were as bewildered as I.

We stopped and exited the car to gawk. The ash was caustic, biting exposed skin on my legs and arms. Breezes made small particles airborne. We probably should have worn masks. In the midst of family, I spoke silently to the Lord. He responded by impressing His message on me.

"Lord!" I shouted in silence. "This is such destruction!"

"The earth is not intended as permanent." His words hit me as the ash. Painful learning. Ripping away my ignorance.

"Lord, this is painful."

"It is painful because you have the perspective of a human. You see nothing, where you should see much."

"I'm overwhelmed with dead trees and animals and people, Lord. Overwhelmed."

"It was this mountain's time to erupt. It builds."

"Builds? It looks like it's been torn apart."

"It's cyclic. Look by your shoe."

I squatted to see a tiny start of a fireweed plant next to the toe of my shoe. In this place of death and destruction, there was a tiny little fireweed digging its roots into the caustic ash and sending its stem up towards the light. The beginning of a new forest.

I reached down touching a tiny leaf and prayed. "May your kind begin to replenish this forest. May your offspring and the new forest grow for a very long time." Though addressed to the fireweed, my prayer went to the Lord.

We left and drove down to the Toutle River near Interstate 5, the highway that runs from Washington State into California. We could see evidence of silt left behind as residue on the leaves of trees marking the high level of water that had raced down from the mountain and under the bridge during the eruption when glaciers melted in an instant. There was a silt-covered beach. Randy, our kids, and I walked on the cool surface at the water's edge. Suddenly with no warning, my right leg was yanked backward hard by super-fast, thick, silt-filled water we'd not known was there. My right foot flapping under the surface as a fish tail. I had dropped into quicksand well over my knee. Randy heard the funny noise I made and pulled me out, and we raced for solid land. We yelled to the kids to go up to the bank to get off the silty beach and out of danger.

I thought sinking into quicksand was a slow, laborious process. Now I knew why it was called quicksand. If Randy had not been there, my body would be buried in the Toutle River silt probably on the other side of I-5 as my body was being pulled so swiftly. I was surprised there were no quicksand caution signs now that the public was allowed to re-enter the area.

"I am still shocked. Lord, I could have died!" It had been an emotionally draining day.

"You cannot die. You have something to do for me."

"Now?" I wondered, feeling empty inside.

"The time is not yet."

For once I was grateful to hear those words.

"So," I laughed silently, "I'm immortal, until I get the work done that the Father plans for me?" I was being silly; He was being serious.

"You begin to see."

"You led Randy to be close by and to hear me and to save my life?"

"Yes."

"Thank You."

A tiny shred of light entered my world. The Lord was there involved in every single part of my life. So much closer than I thought. Some of our interactions we consider coincidences. We are blind to crucial elements woven into the fabric of our future lives when the outcome was planned in the far distant past. When the time is right, the interaction occurs. Everything needed is there. Randy grabbed my arm at the precise moment I needed help. I couldn't perish in quicksand because I had work to do for God. Randy didn't know that.

* * *

A few nights later, I'd shared this experience with my friend Lily.

"Bonnye, you really don't believe in coincidence?" she asked me.

"I see events such as Randy at that river to save my life—I see that as requiring planning, not chance. There is a mind involved. Chance has no mind."

"Do you think God cares about me like that?" Lily drilled a hole into me with her eyes.

"Without question."

"How can you say that with such assurance?"

"Because we are friends. God never wastes anything. He would not waste our time on each other if there were no reason. I believe He is reaching out to you."

Lily's eyes registered surprise. Serious surprise.

Words escaped from me soundlessly. "Lord, please, capture Lily for eternity with You. I'm asking in Jesus's name and for His sake. Amen."

"You say that because you kinda sorta sense something?"

"Yeah, Lily. I 'kinda sorta' sense something. Not to mention I pray for it."

Lily's eyes registered surprise.

I smiled. "My Friend, we promised not to proselytize each other. We never mentioned praying."

She thought for a moment and then laughed out loud. "You are funny! You are really funny. I'm glad we're friends."

"Me too."

Blake Barrett—Tempting Satan

The phone rang, waking me from a deep sleep. It was the summer of 1983. Struggling with the phone, I managed to say hello.

"Bonnye, it's Blake." Blake was someone known to the family, but as I consider it now, I don't think I ever really knew Blake.

I sat straight up at the fright in his voice.

"Bonnye, I was fooling around tonight. I told Satan, 'Show me what you got!'"

"You what?" It must have taken me at least five seconds to say those two words! I couldn't believe what I was hearing. Every hair on the back of my neck stood up straight.

"I thought it was a joke, so I said, 'Show me what you got!' Now my house is freezing cold. A weird cold, I'm totally creeped out, and my wife and I are scared out of our wits. There's something here. Can you make it go away?"

I was wide awake. "I'll see what I can do. Call me when it's gone."

"Father in heaven, help me, guide me, please end this." I had no idea how to help Blake and his wife, but he'd called for help, and he surely needed it.

I stepped into my slippers and turned on the light. I headed down the hallway that would take me to my living room which had a rug. Mom's house where I lived was huge. There were fifteen rooms and I occupied the lower level of the house. For fighting prayer, I needed to be on my knees, and my knees couldn't handle hard floors.

I was filled with the Holy Spirit and felt myself expand. An odd feeling but not unfamiliar. My spiritual size brushed against the walls of the hall—eight feet between walls.

It occurred to me that David, when he met Goliath, must have had this same feeling so that his size, though visibly small, was spiritually huge, since physical size and spiritual sizes may vary for a time in people. That rock he hurled at Goliath couldn't have missed if he was filled as I was being filled.

I had been prepared for war.

In the living room, I lowered myself to my knees on the rug, and began to pray. Often when I pray it's as simple as talking to a friend. This was different. I remained still at the feet of my heavenly Father. I had to get a right heart. Very slowly, word by word, I uttered a prayer of force, not mine, but touching the heart of my Father. This endeavor took words from the very pit of my being for what felt like a long time.

The words came with more strength than I personally have, but God provided. The Holy Spirit enabled me to express the need.

"My holy, heavenly Father, Blake has done something unimaginable. He invited Satan in and, of course, Satan accepted. Only You can fight this fight and remove that evil spirit from Blake's house. You have power over Satan. Use me to help in any way I can. Please remove that evil spirit from Blake's house, Father, and let no other spirits fill the gap he leaves behind. Forbid Satan to return and let Blake realize that it is You who removed Satan and restored peace that he may worship You. End this danger that Blake started. I ask this as a gift, Father, in the name of and for the sake of Jesus Christ. Let Blake be Yours."

For a long time after the words left my heart, I poured out love from my heart to my Father's heart. I could feel it flow. I knew I was heard, and that He would answer my prayer.

Finally, the phone rang.

"It's gone," Blake said. "I've never been so frightened in my life!"

"Don't ever try that again. God made Satan leave you. You need to thank God." My words were flat. I was so tired.

"I won't try that again, and I'll thank God. G'night."

I returned to my room, the spirit within me still brushing the walls in the hall. Sleep would not come. I was too filled. I had to wait until the spirit dissipated before I could return to sleep. I climbed into the Lord's pocket and communed wordlessly in joy over His answer to prayer.

Crossing Chasms

My friend Lily and I both had chasms to cross. Interestingly, they occurred near the same time. Each of us understood the crossing of the other, but it was not something we dwelled on in conversation.

Lily was first of all my friend. I had known her for a couple of years. We had one basic difference—a huge difference. We believed two different things entirely. Lily was into a religion called eckancar. What she described to me sounded like a method of steps to prove one's worthiness. Worthiness to whom, I never really understood. It almost sounded like to self, which struck me as some kind of circular reasoning. Then there was my question, worthiness of what? We talked briefly about what we believed. Not deeply. We agreed that we wanted to be friends but proselytizing was not going to be allowed to enter into what we did as friends. Consequently I cannot answer my questions as to what in her belief was considered worthy. Thanks be to God, I don't have to make myself worthy. Because I also know, I can do nothing to justify myself to God. "Being justified by faith, we have peace with God through our Lord, Jesus Christ."* He justifies us. This tiny little verse is what changed Martin Luther from Catholicism to a reformed belief in the efficacy of faith, not works.

Lily was a special friend whom I really enjoyed, and she was nearing the end stage of a battle with the beast of breast cancer. I hoped to find a way to reach her, but we'd made rules about proselytizing. Lily called and asked me to come visit. She'd recently moved to Kent, Washington, near my home. She said she felt better and would enjoy some reading material if I had anything ready for a beta read. She had been reading my first attempt at a novel.

We sat together in her living room. From her recliner, she asked, "Have you reached the part where you start working on Sam and Felicia? I've wondered a lot about that. I'm curious about what they're supposed to learn, and, also, I wonder whether there is something in that story that would be helpful for me."

Even though we'd made that agreement, I'd still use anything to slip in the Christian message. Sharing my fiction writing with her was legitimate to try to reach her, I decided.

"Funny you should mention that. That's the last story within a story in that package. I just began writing that piece. It's not fully finished, definitely first draft. Here's what I've got." I walked over and laid the bag of papers on her chair-side table.

"That's fine with me. Gives me something pleasant to occupy my mind. Want some coffee?"

"Great. Stay put. I'll get the coffee. You want some too? How you doing, really, tell me without protecting me from the tough stuff in the telling?"

After starting the coffee pot, I returned to the living room and sat on the edge of the sofa.

"There are some times when the pain is so severe, I shout out loud. Since I live alone, there's no problem. It's tough, but I can handle it—so far."

"I'm so sorry you have to go through all that. Is there anything I can do? Anything you want that I can make happen?"

---

* Romans 5:1.

Lily laughed. "Yeah. I know you don't like cooking. You can, however, make a mean enchilada. Could you bring some? We can sit out back to eat while the sun sets."

"Of course. I'd be delighted. When you wanna do it?" I was grateful to have something to do to give her a chance to smile— even if a fleeting smile. I got up to get our coffee.

"Will you check the weather and find a warm evening? That'll be good timing."

"I'll do it and email you the when. If that's not a good time, lemme know."

"Okay."

* * *

Lily had a wonderful view from her deck. A table and a couple of chairs were just outside her slider doors. The Cascade Mountains stood out in a regimental line against a late summer's sky. You could easily see Mt. Rainier rising powerfully above the other peaks. I finished my coffee, took my cup to the kitchen, and stared at the mountains for a few moments. Then I noticed that Lily had drifted off to sleep. She had little time left on this earth, and I didn't want to waken her by opening the door, so I sat on the sofa and mused again about becoming God's vessel, something I desired with all my heart. Something I considered I was born to be.

I had spent my adult life being responsible for my two adopted children and myself and anything else that I felt God wanted me to contribute. I was driven to perform well at my job, being a mother, and living what I thought was a godly life. Lily stirred and woke up. I decided to leave while she was still awake. She was such a great friend. As I drove home, I thought for perhaps the millionth time, I didn't want to lose her, but I knew it wouldn't be long before she was gone. I experienced premature grief.

I took care of fixing dinner and watched the news. I was experiencing some fatigue so I went to bed early. As I slept that night, I began to dream. I was in a dense forest at high elevation following a path to a deep chasm. In the dream, I looked down while holding onto a tree. My head swam with vertigo—it was so far down. A rope bridge spanned the chasm. The slats looked fragile as if they'd break if I stepped on one.

"Father, what are You doing with me?"

With no response, I considered the purpose. "Cross the bridge" was impressed on me unspoken, but as clear as if He had shouted. I knew, of course, He was right there.

I woke, sat straight up in bed, and tried to rid myself of the memory of the experience. I'm not familiar with dreaming. If I dream, I never have more than a shadow of it—unless it's something like this. Something I told myself, as I dreamed, I needed to remember.

I reminded myself that questions such as, "Have you lost your mind?" are not appropriate to use toward God in any of His forms. Still, every emergency signal screamed that bridge is unsafe! I couldn't say things like that anymore. I chose to dive under the pillows to escape and found myself dreaming again. Back at the chasm, I examined the bridge. I wondered if it would turn to dust if I touched it. I wanted to throw up my hands in frustration and stomp around. But again, I knew that was immature, not to mention inappropriate, especially for someone who wanted to belong to God.

The bridge didn't cross the creek perpendicularly to the land. It went off from where I stood to the right at about a twenty-degree angle—enough to look wrong. Maybe the creek ran along an earthquake fault, defined by a little creek way down below or whatever it was at the bottom of the chasm. Maybe a river. It was hard to tell what really lay below as high up as I was and with so much vegetation. I studied the bridge, which appeared as an immense problem. I was certain that to cross required faith, not judgment.

Everything told me it would be suicide to try to cross that bridge. The laws of nature told me not to take such a frightening risk. Here, though, I wasn't dealing with the world and its thought patterns. This was the holy God, and He was Spirit—and I was convinced I wanted to become His useful vessel. All of my thoughts felt awkward. At times, I shifted to the spiritual world, but I wanted assurance that my physical body could go across the bridge, not my spiritual one. Faith cannot demand logical, provable data. I had to remind myself repeatedly.

The Lord's wonderful laugh came to me from the other side of the chasm. I didn't share the laugh. What held me back was earth knowledge, not Godly wisdom.

I walked to the edge of the chasm. I took off my shoes thinking I could perhaps make the crossing better with bare feet. I tied the laces of my shoes together and hung them over my shoulder. I hardened myself to fear and vain thoughts of what could happen. I tried to dial up my faith. God had carefully been teaching me not to fear. For me, learning fearlessness is easier imagined than accomplished.

My safety was in His hands. I pretended I had blinders that shuttered my peripheral vision. I grasped the ropes. My last thought before I put my first foot on that rope bridge was that if the bridge collapsed, I'd get my desire from age six—I'd be in Heaven. First one foot and then the other, I stood shaking, holding onto the ancient-looking rope. The bridge held my weight. I was determined to control my shaking as if that would make the bridge hold me better.

I refused to permit negative thoughts to generate. I crossed the bridge, one foot slowly after the other. Reaching the other side, I fell to the ground. A great creaking noise shattered the silence. I rose up on an elbow to see what happened. The rope tied around the large rock on the other side of the bridge had broken and a large dust cloud was rising. The rock fell into the chasm as if chasing the rope bridge.

While the rope still hung from the near side, I listened to the rock bounce along the wall of the chasm as it descended. The near side of the bridge detached and the bridge fell. Instead of reaching my side of the chasm, it dissolved. Yeah, dissolved. I crept to the edge of the once bridge support. With it and the vegetation gone, I could see a lot better. Way, way down there was a river or creek.

I wanted to scream, "Can't You just once teach me like people do?" Okay question. Presented in wrong attitude. Some vessel I'd make.

I didn't scream. In the middle of the night, I had crossed a rickety bridge over a high chasm, only to see ultimately the bridge—dissolve! There was no return from where I had gone. I had crossed over something. Maybe in time, I'd learn what. Or was this crossing a sign I'd become His or maybe a test of my resilience? He was God; I would be His. He knew all things. In the spiritual world, my brain was essentially still pretty much a blank page.

I kept running the visions through my mind. "Father, did you just test my obedience and faith?" The gentle touch I felt on my shoulder left me no doubt. Of course, my Presbyterian part made my question irrelevant. I knew He knew what I'd do. We'd walked side-by-side on the path that led from the bridge. I must have faith. God had planned all this. He was in control. I need not fear. What, I wondered, had I just left behind? It seemed to me it was everything I already knew, each step was now new.

For so long, I had pursued the Lord. He rewards those who diligently seek Him. Was this a reward? Nah. Such a horror couldn't be a reward, could it?

The next day after work, I meditated on the difference between knowledge and wisdom. Knowledge is man's product; wisdom comes only from God. That was basic. There was a piece of scripture that described what was happening, but I only meditated on part of it. Here's the section from the King James Version of the Bible:*

> My brethren, count it all joy when ye fall into various trials, knowing this, that the testing of your faith worked patience. But let patience have her perfect work, that ye may be perfect and entire, lacking nothing. If any of you lack wisdom, let him ask of God, who giveth to all men liberally, and upbraided not, and it shall be given him. But let him ask in faith, nothing wavering. For he that wavered is like a wave of the sea driven with the wind and tossed.

My focus rested on the second half. The Lord had been patiently teaching me to see what was human to see but not see. He was teaching fearlessness but I was having difficulty getting it. I should have been ready for something that would test me seriously. Although maybe it was just as well that I was ill-prepared. I had nearly passed the faith test, so I let it be. He saw I had faith. Did I waver? Indeed! As a mini earthquake, I wavered in horror at what I was doing, but I did it. I wondered if that counted to Him as faith. I didn't think so. I saw my faith wavering as a candle flame in a stiff intermittent breeze.

---

* James 1:2-6.

The world's knowledge is flat. As much as we have accumulated, it is still flat. God's wisdom has no bounds, being of the Spirit. I see all He says as holding tiny bits of His wisdom, and I longed for more. As He fed me wisdom, I'd dive the depths in awe of what He'd share by diving into the facts I'd been shown. I'd analyze those facts and notice the differences between those facts in a spiritual world and physical world, for they didn't always match. When I had understanding there, I'd surface to spend time astounded by God and His phenomenal differences. At other times, I'd fly to the heavens in ecstasy, enraptured by the beauty and new understanding. At times, the breadth of all He shared would leave me completely in wonder. He enlarged monstrously, and I shrank more and more each time. It was wonderful to have a God so immensely complete. God's wisdom is not flat. It carries with it length, breadth, height, depth of understanding. It does help to be able to see, and I still failed most of those vision tests unless I had help. It certainly kept me humble in a good way.

A few days later, I was downstairs alone and was overcome with the most amazing experience. I was surrounded with understanding of the profundity of the sacrifice Jesus made for me on the cross. It was as if the Holy Spirit could teach me in other ways, reaching my feelings with greater ease and including them in whatever the lesson was. He showed me more and more of the glory of Christ not just in intellectual understanding but also in what I'd have to describe as His showing the glory so I could see in more spiritual depth. I collapsed to my knees in prayer, but my words were jumbled, so I simply poured love out from my heart. It was all I could do, for this intensity of life for the moment was virtually paralyzing.

From deep within my soul, at the farthest corner, my little voice said, "Father, I finally understand what worship is. I thought it meant singing and talking about what a great God You are. Praising Your glory; knowing what Christ did for me. It also meant contributing to the church. Now, I get it. I have nothing to give You. My things are but dust or rust or worse. All I have to give is me. Nothing could have made me happier than that You are part of my life. I have striven to become Your vessel of honor. I have meditated long on this. Please make me Yours. I'm weak and wobbly, but surely there is time in my world to grow."

I knew better than to pray for patience. The way you learn patience is through tribulation. No thanks. I hadn't realized, however, that becoming the Lord's was nearly the same thing from time to time.

"You are certain you want to do this?"

"Father, from before my solid memory of things, I've pursued You. My joy in life is tied to You. My pursuit of You has made my life different from those people in my life and definitely among strangers. I belong with You, not here." With the word here, my arms went out to show the world in which I live. "You said, 'Ask, and it shall be given you; seek, and ye shall find; knock, and it shall be opened unto you.'* Father, through access provided by Jesus, I'm asking, seeking, and knocking."

"I have watched. You are ready for this. You have been doing what I require already. You will have to burn a sacrifice on your altar first."

"What?"

"No one of Mine ever asks Me whether I've lost My mind when I tell them to do something. You must repent of that. It is out of the bounds of propriety. Unless you agree to that demand, you are not ready."

"Father, when I look over my life, it appears to me that to be Yours is why I was born. I know that suggesting You are bizarre is wrong, and I agree to burn that thought upon my altar."

"Very well. You are Mine." He reached into His garment and pulled out a bag, untied it and reached inside. He brought out something on His fingers, rubbed His fingers together, and moved His fingers onto my scalp through my hair, putting something on my head.

It was not a complex process—almost perfunctory. It had no effect that I could detect. The process was quiet, fast, and simple. Not like becoming a member of the body of Christ. The only change I recognized was that I was sure I was now God's vessel, and I was where I was supposed to be, ready to do what I was told to do. This was the most significant change in my life I could imagine. I had crossed my chasm.

* * *

---

* Matthew 7:7-8.

Two weeks after becoming God's, at the beginning of 1988, or at least that's when I knew it, my body could stand it no longer. Problems caused by absorbing a year's worth of low-level toxics from a remodel exploded in my body. I experienced instant asthma; my nervous system went haywire while my brain's electrical system was experiencing a severe destructive event. A run-in with certain substances could cause unbelievable pain in my belly. Sitting at my desk at work talking to Frank, the Personnel Officer, something happened completely beyond my control, my leg jumped and my shin hit the corner of the metal desk with great force creating a hideous bruise. Frank, who had observed what was happening, said to contact my doctor to see if I was okay. I did. I gave myself to God, and two weeks later I was poisoned!

After a few more weeks of seeing one doctor after another, it was clear that at least for a while I needed to remain at home away from substances at work that were triggering the symptoms.

Was my future at work gone? What? And why? Crossing the chasm took my former life and showed it for what it was. I had been thinking I did things by myself and now I had a certain knowledge that God had been holding me up, helping me all along.

And that recognition sharpened my vision in ways I'd tried to sharpen it before but had failed. I was in a new level of my spiritual world.

I learned that the Personnel Officer job had opened up, Frank was retiring, and I was a super candidate. I had run successfully a small but complete Navy agency in the past, my latest review was Outstanding, and in the Army Career Program, my rating for Personnel Officer was Exceptional. I was already budgeting for my Personnel Office expecting to get the job. I was getting a good picture of what chasm I crossed.

"Father!" I cried out, "I didn't have any idea the dream meant that I was essentially a blob of protoplasm, depending on You to make it so I can stand. I had thought I learned to stand as a ten-month-old."

He looked at me oddly. "The concept of a blob of protoplasm does not tie to whether you are employed to work or are Mine. I choose to hold you up to ease your life. Do you wish to rescind your offer?" He asked me.

"Of course not, Father. It's just that I see so much clearer now."

Shower of Roses

I was taught that roses are blessings from God. Georgia Hamilton is the only person I ever found who lived in the physical and spiritual worlds as I do. It was wonderful to be able to share with her.

Mariah, a young family friend, walked to her car, holding Phil, her son, by the hand. Denise, Mariah's daughter followed, occasionally dropping and stopping to retrieve one of the plushy animals she'd brought with her. I had been babysitting them while Mariah went to the dentist.

Mariah's words still rang in my ears. "He wants to save my sins." I had asked her if she believed Jesus was her savior and, if so, why? I'd known her for a long time, and she had studied the Bible with our family briefly. Mariah was into easy answers, and she gave me the same comment she'd memorized wrongly and repeated since childhood, "Of course! He wants to save my sins." A bit short-tempered.

I responded as always. "He doesn't want your sins, Mariah. He wants to save you." I was unable to reach her. She believed she believed. Her response satisfied her. It hurt me. She was a person with a great but sometimes misguided heart. I was a squeaky wheel to her. She was so young. At twenty-two, she was half my age. She had lots of time, I hoped.

Watching her drive away, I looked to God.

"Follow Me," my Father said in a quiet voice. I went to the kitchen, tossed the towel I still carried to the counter, and followed in the spirit. We went out by the back door. I struggled to keep up.

Sometimes God appeared in the form of Jesus—a man—and sometimes as God, the Father. When He represented Himself as a human, He was Christ, and I referred to Him then as Christ or Jesus or Lord. I would call the God representation of the Father, Father.

The hill we climbed was steep and the footholds were a stretch. He stopped, gesturing for me to continue. He took my hand to help me make the last steep step of the climb. I needed it. The final step easy for Him but a challenge for me. We reached the top of the hill. It was a level place where the surface was not dirt and grass but a perfectly still, seemingly solid lake the color of dark sapphire. At the edge on the right another hill rose. I gawked. Inside the sapphire color of the lake were white swirls. Some swirls appeared deeper in the lake than others so that I could not make out their shape clearly. I could stand on the sapphire, which was solid but if I walked out a little way, the solid turned to shallow water deepening gradually. Solid to liquid. But not frozen. My thoughts were distracted, drifting into the amazing solid/liquid transition.

We approached the cave where we often met from another angle. Our normal approach was on the other side of the hill, down from the entryway. The cave was hidden within the hill. From this side, there was a broken tree at the hill. Something white hung from the tree branch almost to the ground. We climbed up to enter.

The cave was white inside. Not even a tiny spider could hide anywhere on the wall or chair. Inside the cave, the floor was small and made of the same sapphire material, solid. It was a very spare room. There was a huge chair with two steps up. He rested His feet on the second step. It was where He always sat when we visited together there. The chair and steps were one solid base. The chair had a flat seat with arm rests and a back that reached above His head. He looked out from there out the cave entrance toward a large body of water, like a distant view of the ocean from atop a hill.

The representation of God as Father was about the size of the statue of Lincoln in the Lincoln Memorial in Washington where Lincoln would measure twenty-seven feet in height if he were standing. The Father's hair was brilliant white, growing just past His shoulders. It grew into pointed ends as if energized by a phenomenal living force in the shape of flames. At night, He must light up the place. He had thick eyebrows, an unshaped beard—full and long. He wore a white leather tunic that fell to His ankles. I wondered what animal it came from as it appeared to be from a single hide. He was barefooted. I wondered how He climbed that hill barefooted. It was all so real, but I knew the image of Him was spirit-designed to prevent damage to me from seeing Him as really He was, while it did give me a sense of Him.

I climbed the steps—they were too tall to step up—and walked to His left knee. At the beginning of the meeting, I embraced His knee, and looked at His face. I was tired from the climb. He gently touched my head and restored my energy.

"What troubles you?" He asked.

I wondered whether I should tell Him. Would I anger Him?

"Speak."

"I'm overwhelmed with the holiness here, Father. I'm unsure whether to say what hurts my heart."

"I said to speak."

"My heart has been troubled over trying to reach Mariah. It hurts me to think that she is not yet Yours."

"I know of your concern. Continue."

"Father, I love You with my whole heart. I desperately want to be in the place You've prepared for me. But, Father, with my concern for her, would You please let me take the separation from You and have You make her Yours? She has a good heart and her need for You is great."

"Stop." The word stuck in the solid sapphire floor like a sharply thrown dagger lands in dirt.

I looked at the face of my Father and felt terror. His white hair and face flamed from red to orange to yellow—colors emanating from Him as fast and hard as lightning. Blue and purple appeared. I was beyond panic-stricken. He reached down and picked me up.

He stood with me stiff as a branch in His hand. We flew. He carried me in the Spirit to a large desert. He stood upon a tall sand dune and set my feet on the hot sand and disappeared. I had never in my life been so frightened. It is one thing to be abandoned, but to be abandoned in an unfamiliar place with no knowledge of where to go was devastating.

Wind whipped up. I fell to my knees. It was a hot wind and full of sand. It pelted my skin, tearing at it, getting into my ears and nostrils, causing blood to break through the surface of my thin skin. I didn't cry, I simply endured until I lost the fear. Like Abraham when his son was to be a sacrifice, Abraham eventually lost his fear. He knew God. He knew God had a plan. That fact gave strength to my seed of faith. Abraham knew God and had faith. God provided a substitute sacrifice. Abraham's faith was rewarded. Perhaps God would reward mine.

At last, the wind died down but nothing happened for a long time. Finally, my heavenly Father picked me up and returned us instantly back to the cave. I stood there, a sandy mess while He no longer showed hot colors.

"Walk around behind me." He pointed to His right. "Bathe in the lake. Clothing has been left for you. Then, return here."

I did exactly as I was told. Not for one split second would I cross Him. I returned with wet hair, wearing a white woolen garment made of two rectangles sewn at the shoulders and sides which fell to mid-calf. The water healed the open sores that had bled from the pelting sand. I knelt at the base of the steps.

"Know this," He thundered. "I will have mercy on whom I will have mercy. Do not ever again reject My gifts to you."

I didn't dare move.

"You gave yourself to Me. Do you wish to rescind your offer?"

"Never, Father. Never." Of that, I was sure. I'd just been tested, I was certain. I wanted nothing more on this earth than to be His useful vessel forever. And I had blundered badly by too little knowledge of Him.

"Stand facing me and take two steps back."

I did.

"Observe." From above us, pieces of rose plants, flowers, leaves, stems, thorns, roots, dirt showered down. It made a dirty pile around me on that sapphire floor so that I could not have walked without stepping on thorns. Bits of the plant and dirt adorned my hair, tunic, and skin.

I didn't move.

"What is the significance of this?" He asked.

"You know that I don't know." Dismayed, I pulled a thorny leaf from the shoulder of the tunic and flicked it to the floor.

"You have to learn how to learn."

I lowered my head. I was supposed to learn. Instead, the plants and dirt just looked to me like a mess that needed to be cleaned up. My mind drifted.

"Focus," He said sharply.

I looked at my Father's face.

"I have just showered you with blessings."

"What?" I was certain I hadn't heard correctly what He said.

"I have just showered you with blessings," He said slowly.

"I don't understand."

"You don't understand because you reason too shallowly."

"What?"

"Consider the rose plant, dirt and all, as a blessing from me. Consider the flower, it has a delightful fragrance and lovely bright color. It's a blessing. Consider the thorny stem and leaves with the thorns even on the underleaf. That's a blessing. Consider the roots and the dirt. They are blessings also. But in your shallow way of thinking the thorns are curses. Am I right?"

"Of course. Who'd see a thorn as a blessing?"

"Someone who could learn from the lesson of the thorn."

I glanced down at the thorny leaf that I'd flicked to the floor. I could identify it because it landed between me and the encircling plant parts and dirt. I bent down, lifted it, and replaced it on the tunic.

"Oh." I looked up at Him.

There was the faint hint of a smile. "I have been and will continue to be showering you with blessings for the rest of your life. Every single thing that happens to you is a blessing from me to you. It is your destiny to reason how the things you would have seen as curses are blessings. Do you understand?"

"I do understand. Some of the things that have seemed harsh to me will be hard to see as blessings."

"Regardless of how hard it may seem, I tell you now that I shower you with blessings. You are to consider each of the thorns and dirt carefully. Do not consider them curses for they are not. Be grateful for all that occurs. All! You are not allowed to despair or feel sorry for yourself or your people. You are to stand up to every event and thank me. I expect it. Do it even if you fail to see or feel it. If for no other reason, do it from respect. It will become habitual. But know that there is a blessing there. If you need help to see the blessing after you have sincerely sought with all your might, ask me. Unless you recognize the blessing, you cannot show gratitude. Otherwise, simply accept what I have said, for I speak truth. To be effective, you must be positive. Know that I am there with you through every event."

"I understand what You've said. I hope I can learn this well for it seems filled with the possibility of failure."

"You will fail sometimes. But you will pick yourself up immediately and start again. There is one other reason I met with you today. I want your promise always to recognize whether you see the blessings immediately or not."

"You have my promise." What else could I say?

He reached down with both His hands and lifted me up to the place where His pocket would be. He placed His palm on my back so I could rest still. This experience pushed me hard, spiritually. I needed desperately to decompress. Warmth coming from His hand calmed me. Going through these experiences was not fun, but I wouldn't change what I was gaining for all the lack of stress in the world. I put my hand on His beard only to discover it was unexpectedly soft on my fingertips. For a brief time, I slept. When I woke, I was refreshed and back home in my room.

Had it all happened? I wondered, looking at my skin. I realized I still wore the garment He had given me. I quickly changed into jeans and a shirt and hung the white woolen garment in the back of my closet. It had happened. It wasn't a dream. There was a token of physical reality in my closet.

I had just learned that He will have mercy upon whom He will have mercy, and He showers whom He chooses with blessings. Everything in my life was a blessing. Everything. Simple words. Huge concepts for me to get my head around.

I no longer have the garment. I didn't want anyone to see it and start asking questions. How could I explain that? I wasn't about to lie. I wondered what I should do with it. It occurred to me to take it to a thrift store. I was convinced that someone needed it and could find it there. Whoever found it and bought it would make good use of it. I would never turn loose of the lessons of that day. And I knew—somehow, I was certain—that He'd save Mariah. No more worry. All was a blessing.

I was also assured that He'd meant for Lily to hear about the Shower of Roses. I picked up the phone and called to tell her what I understood about the Shower of Roses.

My Father in Heaven never tells me anything for someone else. He can reach anyone He chooses. There was no reason for me to be in the middle. I don't even ask because to me it is a sacred thing when He communicates.

It was His choice to tell me to tell Lily that the Shower of Roses applies to her as well. I picked up the phone.

"Hello, Lily. What time are you visitable tomorrow morning?"

"Ten, ten-thirty."

"I wrote a new part of my special book and my Father said to share this one with you since it's for you as much as for me."

"That's exciting. What's it called?"

"Shower of Roses."

"Interesting! I can hardly wait."

* * *

The next morning, I arrived with the manuscript.

"How about if I read this to you, Lily? I don't want you reading for errors."

"Okay." Lily tossed a quilt on her recliner. "I'm getting some coffee. Want some?"

Once we were settled, I read the Shower of Roses piece to Lily. At the place where Father deals with the need to recognize all these rose encounters as blessings, I looked up. A tear silently made its way down Lily's face. My heart clenched, but I kept reading.

I finished and there was incredible silence.

Lily cut through the silence at last. "What will you do with the woolen garment?"

"I plan to take it with some other things to a thrift store."

"That makes good sense. Can I drive over sometime soon and just see it? Touch it? Before it goes to the thrift store?"

"Certainly, but even better, how about I drive over tomorrow morning? I'll bring it."

"Yes, please do."

"Can you imagine how I felt after I understood what these pieces of roses were, and I'd flicked one to the floor?"

Lily laughed good heartedly. "I'd have done the same thing or maybe when the shower began, I'd have run for the dust pan and broom."

It was my turn to laugh. "When the shower began in that super bright room, I was barefoot and there were thorns all over the place."

Demon

I lived at Mom's house after Dad had been moved to a nursing home. I had a great day job, had a mother role during the late afternoon and evening, and spent time later at night with Mom watching Nightline with Ted Koppel and discussing the show before I went to bed. Mom had become bedridden from back problems. She needed social time. I began a four-hour-a-night sleep cycle that would last for over four decades.

One night, I slipped into bed, terribly tired, but couldn't sleep. For some reason, my eyes popped open and went to a spot on the wall. There I saw an irregular, super black, roundish shape roughly three feet in diameter. It wasn't easy to judge size in the semi-dark. It was so black in the partial light that it seemed to shine like patent leather, only alive. Very alive. It had jagged white teeth that could have appeared like a happy face, only it wasn't. It was monstrously malevolent. The objective seemed to be to frighten me.

I was extremely tired from work and in no way interested in stupid stuff. I raised myself up to my knees, still in bed and glared at the thing.

"Look," I pointed at it, "I'm not in the least frightened by you. You have a lot more strength than I do, but one thing is certain—I have Jesus Christ protecting me. He has far more strength than you do! I am His! You just messed with the wrong person. How dare you enter here? And a coward at that, waiting until I'm dead tired! Get out of here and never return. This house is out of bounds for you."

A memory came back to me. I'd had to deal with demons earlier in life. Once after completing college, I was seduced to believe that I had completed college, including securing funding, when others had helped me in huge ways after they were touched by God no doubt. I didn't do it myself. Another time was when Blake called me. The Blake event and this one caused my spiritual size to grow fast. My spiritual size took up a lot of space in my little room. The black shape showed sharp teeth, jagged and hideous. It expanded and contracted. It struggled with something. Jesus, I thought.

"Father in heaven," I prayed, "please remove this thing from the house. Make a barrier through which it cannot penetrate. Surround and protect this house from his kind and any others that might try to enter here. Protect all of Yours who live here now and in the future. I ask You this, my dependable God, in the name of Jesus Christ, and for His sake. Amen."

As I prayed, eyes wide open, the thing became smaller and smaller until it vanished completely. As filled with the Spirit of God as I was, I expected it would take time before I could sleep, but I had no trouble at all.

Weeping Whales

In a vision, I saw humpback and gray whales gathered at the Seattle waterfront.

I left work with a skip to my step because the day was beautiful. I was lighthearted, and the Perry Como song, "Seattle," came to mind as I looked at the sky. It's a happy, catchy song about blue skies that I heard in memory heading to my car.

I found myself falling into the spiritual world, a state I can't drive in. I sat behind my steering wheel, opened my window a little, and began to see one of the worst images I ever saw.

The beautiful blue sky began to cloud up and turn gray, gaining darkness speedily. I stood in the spirit with the Lord on a high piece of land overlooking what He identified as Puget Sound. The slanted land had been thrown up as though from a strong earthquake. The clouds collected themselves over Puget Sound, ever darkening. Red, orange, black, and yellow showed through cloud breaks.

The water was disturbed. Its surface color was black with occasional gray and foamy places floated in bunches where I could see unidentifiable things, floating or rising and falling. Bits of red and yellow reflected in the water's scum-covered surface. Numbers of dead fish floated on their sides. I could not tell where I was due to the darkness and the peculiar land form. I was aware of a stench that took my breath away. I put my jacket to my face to try to filter out the odor. Where was I on Puget Sound?

The sounds of moaning and weeping came to me on the breeze from the water, where boats were lined up side-by-side. A mist rose from the land, but I could not take my eyes off the water. It roiled as if boiling.

I looked to the land. It had a familiar feel, but I was certain I'd never seen such a place. Beyond the water, the land rose up in cliffs? Was this an island? What might have served as signals to locations were lost in the darkness of the scene? The view was fascinating in a ghastly beautiful way. I wanted to comfort the source of the weeping which was heart-wrenching.

The Lord showed me how to descend the hill without falling.

"If you were to look," the Lord said, "you would find absolutely nothing left here made by the hand of man. Much made by man used to be here. All of it is gone. You have been here many times."

I wanted to fall to my knees to weep, but it was too muddy. Something terrible had happened here. Something unspeakable. I slid and the dirt stained my pants' leg and covered my clogs.

We reached the lower level of the hill where land met water and headed north. I assumed we headed north because of the location of Puget Sound. As we walked forward, Puget Sound lay on our left. That would put the area where the Federal Building used to be to our right. There seemed to have been an awful earthquake that left surprisingly fierce residuals. I don't know how I knew we headed north, but I knew. I looked back to the hill where we'd been standing. The land was broken up. It was jagged so that some pieces of the land that appeared to have been deep down were now raised up high. I believed what I'd been told and didn't search for anything made by man.

In the surrounding darkness, it was difficult to see. As we walked toward the boats, I began to feel a strange sensation. The weeping came from the area where the boats were. As we drew closer, it was as if a great sword pierced my chest. The boats were not boats at all. The boats were whales. And they cried. Gray and humpback whales lined the edge of the land. Clouds thundered above and lightning streaked the sky.

"Lord, what is this? I went from a beautiful afternoon to this!"

In an instant, I knew where I was. I didn't want to accept what I'd been shown. I wanted to line up with the whales to moan. I released a sob from deep down inside. I was at the Elliott Bay waterfront near where the Federal Building used to be. I worked for years in that building. I'd parked my motorcycle in the basement. The building no longer existed anywhere—not even a tiny piece. The whales were lying where I used to go with my three best friends, Sam Mallory, Georgia Hamilton, and Dan Williams, to eat lunch at the Red Cabbage Restaurant or to get clam chowder at Ivar's.

The Lord said, "No weeping. Control yourself. You see poorly."

"Lord, God, they hurt. They cry."

"They are not whales; the whales are symbols. Use your eyes and your mind. Who would cry over this destruction?"

My mind churned. The vision of tears falling from their eyes weren't really tears. Whales don't have tears. They have an oily substance to clean their eyes. But these whales were crying.

Suddenly I understood. These symbols were arranged at the foot of the former downtown Seattle area. Anything man-made was gone. Utterly gone.

What did the presence of the whales have to do with anything? Did they cry over the wipeout of things man-made? The massive change their eyes beheld? I had my doubts on that. They weren't really whales. They were tightly lined up together. Were the whales representing people? Significantly large people? People of grand stature? I let that settle in.

"Lord," I said quietly, "will this come to be? Is this whole picture symbolic or are the whales the only symbol? You are showing me Leviathans weeping. You told me I needed to study Job and Ezekiel. Job learns of Behemoth conquering Leviathan. Are the whales Leviathans? Job refers to them as a king over all the children of pride. Have they been conquered by Behemoth? Job refers to Behemoth as he is of the ways of God. Like Satan is conquered by Jesus at Armageddon?"

"It comes."

"Will I see it when it comes?"

"No."

That word assured me. "Thank You, Lord. Thank You. Once is enough."

"The whales make you sad. The whales are idolaters. They worship money. Remember, worship of money is the root of all evil. They may seem huge and powerful, but they only fool people as they fool themselves."

"Lord, I have You to teach me to see. The whales don't see."

"They have no excuse," He said with finality, as if He spit the words out. "They rejected truth to burn it on their altars to self."

This vision occurred in the late 1980s. It hurt to see the whales hurt, and it was hard to look at the whales and imagine them as people worshipping money. But it helped me to understand why their view of the torn-up land made them weep. In the later part of the 1980s, I was naïve. I had no clue the extent of corruption that comes with the worship of money—hoarding, comparing personal quantity with others, wanting for more, traitorous behavior, never giving to those in need without payback. Just a few of the endless array of money-worship sins.

I was so naïve. Decades would pass before I actually saw the devastation that "whales" could inflict on others and the land and anything they got their hands on, including me. The spiritual world and the physical world did not always show the same image at the same time. When I finally did see corruption, I remembered the whales and mused back on that vision. And when I finally would see that evil corruption trying to establish itself in the first part of the years in the twenty-first century, this image stands as a reminder to me that vengeance is not ours, and it will be done by the only righteous one. It will be done. And that vengeance will be just and certain, dreadful to witness, righteous in execution. Knowing all that makes it easier for me to forgive, for as Jesus said on the day of His crucifixion, "They know not what they do."

Starting the engine to drive home was difficult after such a vision. I had to sit and decompress first. I felt as if I had just been to the edge of hell.

Beautiful blue sky above me back at my car belied the gray mess I'd just seen at the waterfront. Something that would come to be, but I would not be there when it did. Thank—You—God.

Was I supposed to see that externals in people were sometimes covering what took a long time to recognize for what they really are? That even strong man-made structures are totally temporary? That I walk through a place of constant upheaval though it may sometimes appear peaceful?

Neuropsychological Exam and a Toad

The clinical neuropsychologist I saw in my workup after I'd been poisoned was a wonderful person. When she asked me what I felt guiltiest about, she started to laugh and it was a wholesome open laugh AT me. It didn't bother me. I was certain she'd explain, and she did.

After I'd been poisoned in 1988-89, I had to have numerous neuropsych exams. In the late 1980s, those experiencing poisoning for any reason usually began a medical workup with one neuropsychological exam performed by a clinical psychologist or clinical neuropsychologist or more than one. My first was conducted in Seattle by Eileen McCarty, the second exam was at the Oregon Health Sciences University. She spent two days with me, evaluating my case. These two neuropsych exams were designed to determine whether I had organic damage from poisoning or a psychologic or psychiatric problem. Clinical psychologists and clinical neuropsychologists were medically charged with making that decision. No other medical specialty can make that decision.

Toward the end of the extensive first day of testing, Eileen asked me what was the one thing I felt guiltiest about in my life?

I was stunned. I'd never even considered such a thing, but I knew the answer immediately.

I told Eileen about the afternoon at the creek when I was poking around in the sand with a stick and felt something funny. I dug down and pulled a toad from its hole. I hadn't known they hibernated, but I figured out that was the problem with the stupefied toad. I was horrified. I explained how I tried so carefully to rebury the toad.

"I was heartbroken," I said, "because I never knew whether the toad was okay or whether I'd killed it with my carelessness."

Eileen covered her face with her hands and laughed and laughed. I realized quickly that she was, indeed, laughing at me. She seemed to have trouble containing her laughter. It didn't bother me. I had gotten to know her. She was, through and through, a good and decent person.

After she finally calmed down, she offered an apology.

"Why were you laughing?" I asked.

She leaned back. "Bonnye, I've sat here listening to person after person answer that same question for so many years. I've never, ever heard that one. It is totally unique. What's even funnier is that I completely believe you. The story fits your psyche perfectly!"

"Is that good?"

"It sums up what I have concluded. You have been poisoned. Your symptoms are a result of poisoning, not a psychological or psychiatric issue. And you are still naïve, unsullied by this world. You're refreshing."

Georgia Hamilton and the Angels

Georgia is the only person I ever met who had the same split physical-world/ spiritual-world life that I did.

I was on assignment with a team in Portland, Oregon, evaluating personnel management at the headquarters of the Bonneville Power Administration. I received a phone call from my boss at the Office of Personnel Management telling me a federal agency on the south side of Puget Sound wanted to hire me as head of Classification and Performance Management. I would also have the entire personnel function at Gold Creek. It would add two hours on the ferry to my day when I went to the island, work in conditions that were visually dismal, and dealing with a guy who clearly didn't want me there. It would be a stressful mix. On the other hand, I knew they had problems and needed help. I knew I could help. I told her I'd call her the next day with an answer.

Moments later the phone rang again.

"Hi." Georgia Hamilton sounded tired.

"Well, hello, Georgia. You just get in?"

"Yeah. The train was a bit late today. Want some blue fin tuna?"

"Sounds wonderful. You want to unpack or go eat first?"

"Eat! I'm ravenous."

"I can meet you downstairs in fifteen minutes. Okay?"

"Yes, unless you can get downstairs sooner."

We met and headed out. Georgia did what she always did. Once we exited the hotel, she looked all around before stepping any distance from the entrance. She'd been brought up in New York City.

Our families had raised us extremely differently. She considered me clueless about people and I teased her about being paranoid. She teased me about being a Confederate, and I teased her about being a Yankee. We shared significant experiences. We both lived with one foot in the spiritual realm and the other in the physical realm. We could talk to each other about our experiences. Neither of us discussed our split lives with others.

She waved from her spot near the revolving door. We left and began the walk to our favorite seafood restaurant.

"You know, we probably should have called a taxi."

"Why?" I shoved my purse strap higher on my shoulder. This purse liked to slide down and land with a thud on my forearm. I wanted to search for another.

"See that group of guys?" She pointed ahead of us. "Not sure they're okay."

"Georgia," I said with some forced patience, "look around us."

"I don't see . . . oh, my gosh." She stopped moving altogether. Her mouth dropped open. "You can see right through them. How many are there?" She turned in a slow circle looking up.

"I think six," I said.

"They must be seven feet tall! There are six of them. We have spiritual protection? You may have it for the work you have to do. Nobody told me when I was six that I had work to do for God. If someone had, I'm not sure I'd have taken it seriously, certainly not seriously enough to figure that I was immortal until I got the work done."

"Are you making fun of me?" I asked.

"No. I can hear the voices of those guys. They don't seem to know we're here."

"God uses many tools. He can make people see but not see, hear but not hear. He can surround us with angels. Have faith, my friend."

Georgia held her breath as we passed the men. They appeared to have no recognition that we were there. I would have expected her to have depended on spiritual protection coming from New York City. But we do know that just because your spirit is awake, not all people have the same skills or abilities.

"They didn't see us," she whispered.

A few minutes later we entered the restaurant. It was noisy, their excellent food meant they were often crowded.

We were seated and chose our dinner selections. Our order was taken swiftly.

"I got a call from Lucy Johns," I announced.

"Here?"

I nodded.

"Wha'd she want?"

"She got a call from where I was furloughed last summer. They want to hire me to head Classification and Performance Management at Tuesday Point and run the entire operation at Gold Creek. I told her I'd call her tomorrow."

"You're not going to do it, are you?"

"I don't want to, but their need is great. It's ugly over there. In Seattle, we have gorgeous views from the Federal Building. I'm thinking to create a list of must haves this evening. I'll give her the list and tell her if they meet all my wants, I'll do it. I'm thinking of things like ferry tickets, an office I can close and lock, my choice of employees . . . I'll limit my wants to fifteen. They'd have to build me an office since none currently exists."

The next day I called Lucy with a list of fifteen items they had to guarantee. Lucy assured me that I'd made it clear I didn't want to work there. Very shortly afterwards, I received another call.

"Bonnye, they must really want you over there. They've agreed to every single one of the items on your list. If anyone can make a difference, you may be able to do it."

Georgia and I met for breakfast the next morning. I shared my list of fifteen items.

"I can't believe you did that. Now tell me. Have you heard back from Lucy?"

"Yeah. I have a new job."

"My condolences."

"Thanks."

Nyla, Huge Lesson

My first large assignment for the Lord as a vessel to honor Him involved a former employee of mine who was sick at Harborview Hospital in Seattle. Doctors could not determine what caused a fever that would not go away. God used me there to teach both of us a great lesson.

In Seattle, rain normally mists. A foreign rain fell outside that day. Rain-ducks are little water bodies, created by forceful raindrops that cause a splash in the water and sometimes appear to produce a long neck with a head and a tail. This hard rain made rain-ducks in puddles that had a little depth. Unusual for Seattle, there were many rain ducks that day. Having moved from the east coast, I thought of the rain making ducks as "real rain."

I had been feeling punk for days. I had a fever from a cold and was sneezing constantly. My nose was raw.

When the phone rang, I picked it up and sneezed a good one before I could answer. My voice was raspy.

"That doesn't sound good," said the voice on the phone as I wracked my brain trying to identify the familiar sound.

"No, it isn't good."

"Bonnye, it's Nyla, Nyla Welton. Do you remember me?"

131

"Of course, Nyla. How are you?" Nyla had been one of my clerks when I worked for the government.

"I'm not doing well. I'm at Harborview Hospital. I was hoping you'd be able to visit me here."

"Why are you there?" I asked.

"I got real sick and ended up here. Nobody knows for sure what I've got or how to cure it."

I hated hospitals. Harborview was definitely not somewhere I wanted to go. This day my cold gave me an excuse.

"As sick as I am, there's no way I can go into a hospital."

We didn't chit-chat. She said she'd call back if she remained in the hospital. I hoped she'd get well fast.

She didn't.

She called every other day. My cold dragged on.

After yet another call from Nyla, I felt that familiar pressure on my shoulder.

"You have to go there," my Father demanded.

The next time she called, the cold was waning—it was time. We decided on the next day, and I asked her if there was anything I could bring. She wanted a negligée and romance novels. After I hung up the phone, I groaned. No way. I saw a big red flag.

I worried over what to take, and I was led to plain pajamas and a copy of the New Testament, a little book that fit in my hand. I kept several for whenever they might be needed.

The Lord led me to take up the marker that doesn't soak through Bible pages, and I went through the New Testament for Nyla. I didn't have a clue what verses related to her, but the Lord did. He virtually pointed out the verses to highlight.

That night I got a call from the nurses' station at Harborview. The nurse assured me that her calling was unusual, but Nyla was very sick, and they had had no success in helping her to recover. The nurse pleaded with me to come to the appointment I'd made with Nyla the next day. I assured her I'd be there.

I arrived at Harborview, gritted my teeth, and finally found Nyla's room. She walked to me rapidly and we hugged.

"I knew you didn't want to come, but I need you desperately."

"God is why I'm here."

"I know."

I felt around blindly for the Lord, wondering how she knew.

Nyla and I walked to the visiting room and sat down.

"Bonnye, I've led a terrible life. I've done some awful things. I need to confess these things, turn from them, and never do them again. I need to be forgiven and renewed. I need to be saved."

I screamed spiritually in silence, "Father, this is way, way over my head. It's like not knowing how to swim and being dropped into the deep end of the swimming pool. I know Your Holy Spirit can give me the words to say. You must help me, for this is beyond anything for which I'm remotely prepared.* I ask You in the name of Jesus and for His sake."

Nyla was so sincere. She was so troubled. I ached for her in such spiritual pain. I put my arm around her with a hug and then sat back.

"Nyla, go ahead with what you want me to know. My job is to listen."

I can't repeat what she told me, but I can say that it freaked me out in my utter naïveté. God's Holy Spirit spoke to her through me. He was calm and spoke with my voice as I watched and listened.

As she gave her confession, I wanted to weep, to throw up, to beat my fists on the floor, to tear out my hair at so many inappropriate things. The Spirit closed all that down and took over. I was entranced by how He treated her. It was the loveliest thing I ever saw. He did it through me, as I watched. I stayed awestruck the entire time. She was in pain, terrible pain, and He was going to heal her through me.

As the session continued, I relaxed, grateful that the Lord had seen fit to use me. He was teaching me while He healed Nyla.

When it was finally over, I had Nyla promise me that she'd never fall back into her old ways, and that she'd find a church and stick with it. She promised she would.

I discovered to my shock that I'd been there for five hours. Five hours! Time had flown by.

As I gave Nyla the small bag with her pajamas and the New Testament, I experienced the same sensation I had so many other times. The Holy Spirit had filled me so much that I could feel the increase in spiritual size. We walked to her room and parted. My spirit had never been so large.

I started driving home and began to cry which was unusual.

---

* Luke 12:11-12

"Thank You, Father, for using me. Thank You so much. You could have used anybody, and You chose me. I have never seen such beauty in such misery. I have never had such a task. But what I've been taught and what I've seen is miraculous. Please heal Nyla now. Let her go home to be with her children. And keep her, Lord. Keep her from straying ever again. I ask in the wonderful name of Jesus Christ and for His sake. Amen."

That night Nyla called. She was in tears. "Thank you, so much. The pajamas are a perfect fit. But you've got to know this. I went back to bed with many questions, but the little Bible answered them all and more. It made me remember the old spiritual songs I used to sing. My fever broke. I can go home soon."

"I'm so happy for you. My heart still sings from our time together. It was a lovely transformation."

"There's more. Listen to this. The woman in the bed next to me has been in a coma for a long time. Even so, I asked her if she minded if I sang. She didn't make a sound. I started to sing, and it just poured out of me. Bonnye, the woman next to me woke up while I was singing those old gospel songs, she was out of the coma."

The hair on my arms stood straight up. I could hardly believe what I was hearing.

After we hung up, the nurse who had called me to confirm I could visit Nyla, called and confirmed what Nyla had told me, including the woman coming out of her coma. The nurse told me they certainly could use me there. I thanked her and explained that I could hardly stand being in a hospital.

I rejoiced in God that night. He let me accompany Him as He worked a miracle, a transformation of a human, a gift that continued to give.

Nyla called me once more. She asked me to come to the service when she was becoming a member of a local church. I went, and my joy was boundless. I have not seen her since. But I no longer have worries where she's concerned.

"Thank You, Father. I feel that I've had a real experience as Your vessel. You could have done what You did using an endless array of options, yet You chose to use me as Your vessel. I am humbled beyond beyond. You surely touched my heart at its base and turned the sad into joy. You grew Nyla and me."

Essential Epitome of Equality

Katy and her friend, Susan Rivera, came from Richmond to visit us every other year in Seattle. We had great times exploring the area and beyond. We visited touristy places, but also, we explored the Bible. One night, we stayed at Paradise Inn at Mt. Rainier, and of course, the Bible was with us.

The moon, huge and bright, hung almost within reach at the Inn. The chipmunks, which had been busy inside the Inn all day running up and down the great halls, had disappeared. We sat on the porch and took in the night noises and cool air.

"I wish you could have heard some of the speakers we had at Soup and Sandwich at Church on Wednesdays. There have been some wonderful speakers," Katy said with enthusiasm.

She shared some of the subjects, and they did sound interesting.

When the conversation slowed, I asked, "Do you have a head table at your Soup and Sandwich?"

"Of course," Susan said.

"I learned something new, something I missed for years when reading Corinthians," I said.

"What was that?" Katy asked, maybe wishing she hadn't because she didn't always know where the conversation would take us.

"Who sits at your head table?"

Susan said, "Well, the speaker and the minister and other dignitaries."

The light of the moon reflected in the window so clearly that it was as if we had two moons, one on either side. Katy and I were both so short that we never seemed to find seating places where our feet could comfortably rest on the floor. I was perched on the edge of my chair, slowly swinging my feet to and fro as a cat might gently whisk its tail.

"That's what I've always seen. That's what most churches and non-churches would do in setting up the head table, but in reading First Corinthians, I realized we definitely do some things backwards."

"Who should sit at the head table, then?" Katy asked.

I paused, wondering whether Katy and Susan were ready. "The cook, the dishwasher, and the janitor."

Katy almost lost her coffee. "What?"

"First Corinthians 12 addresses the different members of the Body of Christ, some having more inherent honor than others. It takes all parts to function. But we humans think some parts are more to be honored than others. Listen to this from verses 17 to 22."*

> If the whole body were an eye, where were the hearing?
> If the whole were hearing, where were the smelling?
> But now hath God set the members, every one of them,
> in the body, as it hath pleased him.
>
> And if they were all one member, where were the body?
> But now are they many members, yet but one body.
> And the eye cannot say unto the hand, I have no need of
> thee; nor again the head to the feet, I have no need of you.
>
> Nay, much more those members of the body which seem
> to be more feeble, are necessary.

"That's sort of the preamble. Here's the hammer in verse twenty-three and twenty-four."†

> And those members of the body, which we think to be
> less honorable, upon these we bestow more abundant
> honor; and our uncomely parts have more abundant
> comeliness. For our comely parts have no need; but God
> hath tempered the body together, having given more
> abundant honor to that part which lacked, that there
> should be no schism in the body, but that the members
> should have the same care one for another.

"The key to me is"

> And those members of the body, which we think to be
> less honorable, upon these we bestow more abundant
> honor.

"What a principle! Imagine if we did that as a people!"

---

*   I Corinthians 12:17-22.
†   I Corinthians 12:23-24.

"The idea of seating the cook, dishwasher, and janitor at the head table would never be acceptable at Soup and Sandwich," Susan said. "That's just not how things are done."

I couldn't resist asking why.

"I can't say how many times I've read that passage, but I've never understood it that way. I understand the principle, but it feels unnatural." Katy spoke her thoughts out loud.

I read lines 26 to 28.*

> For ye see your calling, brethren, how that not many wise men after the flesh, not many mighty, not many noble, are called; But God hath chosen the foolish things of the world to confound the wise; and God hath chosen the weak things of the world to confound the things which are mighty; and base things of the world and things which are despised, hath God chosen, yea, and things which are not, to bring to nothing things that are.

"Nobody will ever seat the cooks, dishwashers, and janitor at the head table at Soup and Sandwich. They wouldn't even be comfortable sitting there." Susan was frustrated.

"I'm simply sharing a principle I believe. Your Soup and Sandwich is not my business. I'm just entranced by this principle. I love seeing as God shows me to see. He actually sees all us Christians as absolutely equal. It makes me wonder why even have a head table? Why are not all seated randomly? Why do we have words like dignitaries? Or 'our betters?' God makes it absolutely clear that He sees no person as superior to any other. The verse I think of here is this: "there is no respect of persons with God."† That is, He shows no favoritism to any human."

Silence fell on us. I hadn't meant to shut down our interaction.

Later Katy and I would chew on this idea when we were off to ourselves. She wanted to know how I had come to understand things that scholarly others never seemed to have seen.

I finally—after all the years—told her how the seeds that she planted in me had been cared for by the Lord, that He had never left me but instead taught me through my life. I'd broken a rule that was biblical and parental in choosing to follow Him, yet the Lord

---

*   I Corinthians 1:26-28.
†   Romans 2:11.

had approved. I told her about my vision at age six. He focused His work in my life on seeing. He wanted me to see differently from the way much of the rest of the world sees. He succeeded, though I had far to go.

Porcupine and the Laugh of God

This is one of the many Spirit Houses at the Historical Park and Orthodox Church, Eklutna, Alaska.

We had visitors. People love to visit us in Alaska. They would like to see what we've seen over years of living here—condensed into a two-week segment. Sometimes, it's just not going to happen the way you'd expect or desire.

We had visitors who wished to see a porcupine in the wild. Once my daughter and I had visited Lake Eklutna. As we were leaving and the sun was fading from the Chugach Mountains, we watched a porcupine climb up the hill from the road it had just crossed. It was a fascinating encounter. The quills on its back swayed from side to side like a Hawaiian grass skirt, hula-like, as the animal slowly waddled up the hill. That's the first time I'd seen one in the wild. It was a treat to watch.

Our visitors wanted to duplicate that experience. It was unlikely that such a rare event could be re-created, so I prayed, "Lord, let us find a porcupine this day." Knowing the answer to prayer is "yes," "no," or "wait," I definitely expected a "no" this time, but I didn't say so. I just let the visitors know that it would be significantly difficult to find a porcupine on demand.

We had taken some touristy trips that day. We'd seen everything on the agenda except the porcupine. You just don't see porcupines every day. On the way home, we decided to stop to see the spirit houses at the Eklutna Historical Park and Orthodox Church in Eklutna, a small Native village between Anchorage and Wasilla. It's on the opposite side of the highway from Lake Eklutna at the same turnoff.

We paid the small park fees and took our tourists into the cemetery where the ground is covered in a burst of color and creativity that I've seen in no other cemetery. To me, death should be a celebration of new life in heaven, not a somber event. I loved this place, for it does just that.

This cemetery reflects my view of how I'd like to be buried. There are some graves covered with a blanket or quilt, maybe a favorite of the person whose remains lie there. Some graves are literally built over with little houses, spirit houses, some of which appear to contain possessions of the deceased. One has a cartoon moose statue about four feet tall labeled "Bullwinkle."

I see the cemetery as a way of laying down earthly things. It's personal, unique, happy in a way that a cemetery can be happy. Some spirit houses are very elaborate. Some are surrounded by picket fences. The painting is delightfully disparate—every color of the rainbow! The colors are all juxtaposed in the sense of wildflowers on a hillside appearing to announce springtime. Our visitors were drawn in to the uniqueness.

I reached the end of the cemetery rows first. I looked down, running through my mental checklist for the day, and realized we hadn't seen our porcupine. I hadn't expected to see one. It was broad daylight, not the best time to spot one. I looked up, thinking it was about time to head home.

A recent grave caught my eye. It was a spirit house over the body of Nick Stephan "Porkypine." I laughed out loud.

The Lord chose to show us this Porcupine! Hilarious! I could hear the laugh of the Lord rumble back at me through the trees. And I learned there are four answers to prayer: "yes," "no," "wait," and "one that reflects a sense of humor only the Lord could create."

I tried to share the porkypine, but that wasn't what people wanted to see. Still, I enjoyed it immensely and laughed with the Lord. To me, His laugh on us was worth the entire day of touristy stops. I am likely to remember it as long as I have a memory. It still makes me laugh.

Nick Stephan "Porkypine" you were an answer to prayer. I never knew you, but I'll remember you for the rest of my life.

Restoration

When I asked God to make me His vessel to honor Him, I was pleased that He accepted me. From that time, my life changed dramatically. He began to fulfill what He'd told me He would do, restoring me following the poisoning event that weakened my whole body and affected my brain. I began to be overwhelmed with the restoration as it was far in excess of what I imagined. I rejoiced that He would treat me in such abundance.

In so many ways, the Lord has restored me since the late 1980s when I was accepted as a vessel to honor my God. After I was poisoned, the Lord promised a restoration. He has already abundantly restored me. Three examples: I never had a house of my own; now I do. I never had a business; now I do. I longed to retire and live in Alaska; now I do.

For many old people with breathing problems, the most comfortable place is in a recliner with feet and back elevated. I relax by turning my body into a partial form of a bivalve mollusk. I was sitting in my Alaska home's great room one evening when the Lord appeared. In His appearances, He is the size of a man dressed as is appropriate in the Middle East without the head gear. I scrambled about struggling to get to my bony knees.

I was quite a sight. My hair was ruined when I was poisoned. Without my wig, my head gets cold, so at home I often put on a fuzzy knit hat. It's comfortable then. So there I am with a pink fuzzy hat, my pajamas, and two throw blankets in a recliner with my dog next to me. She guards me with barking when some people come into the house. She doesn't bark at the Lord.

His hand was on my shoulder. "Don't get up. Stay there. I see that you are about to wrap up the book, so I decided to stop by. You finally figured it out. I am pleased."

"You had me do it for me, I think, as much as for any reader."

"You knew the information. I just wanted you to see how it fits together."

"Thank You, Lord. It's really acceptable like this?"

"For this point in the process, yes."

"I want to thank You for Your restoration. When I finally learned what You wanted of me for this assignment, I was overwhelmed. I was still really sick from the poisoning. As I began to work, You grew me and healed parts of me so I could do this work easier. I think the word easier is the wrong word. None of this has been easy. You helped me remember events and details I'd about forgotten for they were so far in the past. You helped me connect things I'd never connected before.

"Not only did You help me do what I needed to do, You fulfilled Your promise. You restored or maybe over-restored me. I own a home. Never in my life did I ever own a home. It's an incredibly peaceful home. I am so grateful. Then, You created 'appointments' where I ran into people I needed to meet. You had it so that both my second daughter and her husband wanted as did I to live in Alaska and to live in part of my house. They help when things are too tough for me. You have truly blessed me with them. You have connected me with two dogs, my comical companions, Sydney and Rika. They enrich my life giving me endless reasons to laugh.

"You've enabled me to travel in this great land to see Your mighty creation. You've shown me doctors who have been wonderful in my life, doctors who pushed beyond what they already knew to provide proper medical care for me.

"You've given me beautiful views whether it's the northern lights gracing my home in winter with their wavy fly overs or whales breaching, sleeping, or singing amplified with the boat's microphones lowered into the water.

"What You've given me, Lord, is overall peace and beauty. It's so special. I rejoice in it all and in You for Your provision. And when I was reluctant to go, You pushed me to see Nyla and have the spiritual experience of a lifetime in that interaction. So many things for which I am enormously grateful, Lord. Some of the things have repeatedly washed over me in joy since they occurred.

"You prevented a heart attack when I was sitting atop one. It required a triple bypass. I expected that I would finish my book after the heart surgery and then maybe talk to a few groups, and then, I hoped, Lord, You'd finally let me walk up those amazing stone steps to find You and my eternal home. Well, that didn't happen yet. You have restored me beyond my expectations. I always found Your generosity amazing. My needs were not only met, but exceeded beyond my wildest dreams."

Then the Lord spoke again. "Your restoration is not yet complete. There is still more to come. There is also more to come on your assignment in relation to the book. You must stop stressing over the book. It is working as it must. I have an interest in this effort or I would not have assigned it to you. Just keep moving through the process. The outcome is Mine."

"I'll try, Lord. In doing this for You, my concerns were numerous and my desire for doing my best ever was primary. I don't remember how many times I'd write half the book and throw it away for not measuring up. I kept remembering You wanted me to share what took place between us. I kept drifting off into the weeds."

"The stress you permitted yourself—has it helped you at all?"

"No, it's put me where I am right now. Exhausted."

"Not good for numbers of reasons."

"True."

"It costs you, when you permit it."

"I realize that, but I'm not good at applying those brakes."

"Then you pay the price until you learn. I will go now. Know that I am well pleased."

"Thank You, Lord."

Afterword

Moonlight reflecting on surface of Atlantic Ocean.

As a young child in both Richmond and Savannah, I would soon learn that the ocean was located in a specific direction, even though I couldn't see the beach. When I faced north and held out my right arm to the side and pointed, that was where to find the Atlantic Ocean. The beach was always east.

I feel a need for geographic orientation. I don't know why. Normally, once I've been somewhere, I know how to make my way home and find the location again. I don't use street names or highway designations—things either look right, or they don't. In the case with the ocean, I knew where it was because we'd driven to the beach often. Other cues were added later. I had a sense of the ecliptic as it would be viewed from Virginia to Georgia, so the position of the sun also offered cues.

In my mind, east and Atlantic Ocean were virtually synonymous. Whether we were in Virginia, the Carolinas, Georgia, or Florida, I knew immediately where the Atlantic Ocean was. When I moved to Seattle that changed, and I was thrown into geographic chaos. I had to substitute the Cascade Mountain Range for east, but I had such a strong water connection that the Pacific Ocean caused confusion. More than once, I drove north when I wanted to go south or east when I wanted to go west because my internal compass was tied to the direction of the ocean. Time and experience changed that, but at first my internal navigation was awkward.

I don't vacation at the Atlantic Ocean or have any desire to go there at this time. What I remember is no longer there. For example, we spent many days at Hilton Head Island, South Carolina, when Dad was stationed at Hunter Air Force Base in Savannah. It was back when the only access to the island was a car ferry. If I remember right, that ferry took less than six cars. Maybe two? I can't remember.

Back then, creeks harbored alligators; residents painted their doors blue in the tradition of "Haint Blue" which is a pigment created by slaves and still used in the southeast low country to ward off evil spirits; deer jumped across the road to avoid cars; no hotels existed; the sandy beach shared space with sea turtles, horseshoe crabs, deer, and cows. For anyone who's been to Hilton Head Island, you realize that as I write this, I'm old. Really old. I'm past the life expectancy for United States women. It has been a long time since Hilton Head saw the variety of wildlife as routinely as I did.

At Hilton Head, we fished in the surf for blue sail cats—a particularly beautiful salt water catfish, watched horseshoe crabs waddle at the water's edge, and saw a sea turtle leave her eggs and return to the sea before swimming off. I had my sixteenth birthday there and observed the occasional large animal meander by between the surf and sea oats. I want to remember it as it was, not how it is now with hotels and golf courses all over the place. I was there at a time when all I could hear were natural sounds.

The Pacific Ocean is lovely, and the western coastline is amazing, but the ocean to which I feel life-connected is the Atlantic. It's the place where I spent the most time with light from the moon and stars creating a road on the water at night. I imagined the splashes of moonlight on the waves were the Lord's footprints as He walked the light road created by His moon. I followed Him spiritually by dancing in His footprints.

In my mind, the moon's path is another type of entrance to my eternal home. It's alluring, and I always knew not to start walking out in the water, but it draws me to the spiritual world to commune and, oddly, to dance. On the light road, I'm free to let my dancing out as a spiritual offering of love to God, my movement following in His footsteps at night. Unseen by human eyes, my physical body waited patiently on the shore.

All the while, the light spray of salt water—life-giving, healing—provides a scent that surpasses all the perfumes on earth. The crashing waves play water music that reaches the core of my soul. It's the tune to which I dance while pouring out love for my Creator. It is as if my chest has an opening through which to expedite praise to my Lord. Though I now live a few mountains away from the Pacific Ocean, when I stand facing north, I know where the ocean is.

The geography is different again now that I live in Southcentral Alaska. I've adjusted to that difference. But little wonder I find this place peaceful. This will be the place from which I eventually ascend the stairs I saw over the bayou seventy-six years ago to reach my eternal home. What a day of full joy that will be for me. I'll shift from north, east, south, west to up. A totally unique location will begin for me.

I'll enjoy this new orientation of up and all that goes with it forever.

About the Author

After decades of working in academia as a public school and homeschool teacher and in business and for the federal government, Alaska author Bonnye Matthews experienced a life-changing event in 1988. She was poisoned. No longer able to work; she was expected to die, a prognosis she strongly rejected. Knowing she had work to do in the future, Matthews decided to write with an aim to prevent or reduce for others the hazards that changed her life. She created two books, the first of which brought communications from nine different readers with a message for which she was totally unprepared—the book stopped their planned suicides.

Early after the millennium change, she moved to Alaska to retire in the clean air of a beautiful place she'd come to love. Further writing never crossed her mind. She took a class at Mat-Su College on Alaska History and became fascinated with the first

Americans. She researched deeply enough to realize that at that time (1) teaching of the arrival of the earliest Americans was not close to accurate (2) nor was the ice-free barrier transit possible. She recoiled that fiction was being taught as fact. That spurred her to write fiction demonstrating the facts she had learned. She'd never written fiction before, and she wasn't an archaeologist. Non-fiction was already covered by academic experts.

Bonnye wrote a five-book novel series and followed that with a three-volume novella series with a focus on specific archaeological sites. She wrapped up that set of books with her peopling of the Americas paradigm. Her series books are listed on the inside back cover.

Her recent book, *Arctic Dinosaurs of Alaska,* contains a middle-grade novel and is chock full of multidisciplinary learning opportunities.

She competed her books to learn more about writing and how to improve. She was surprised, not having taken writing classes, that each of her competed books won awards at state, national, and/or international levels.

Bonnye's life is one where happiness and joy abound. The joy is real—though some wonder how. From early childhood, she learned what Solomon wrote about in Ecclesiastes in the Bible: work is the source of joy. Whether she works to learn something or communicate with others, her motto has been two words her great-aunt Katy Bradley wrote on her soul at the end of World War II: beyond beyond. If giving 80% were the basic standard, giving 100% might mean going beyond. Bonnye would give 120%, because she'd made that level of work habitual. It's where joy is found, she'd explain. She received recognition because of her products, but that was minor compared to the joy she found in the work. That joy is like an internal glow, she'll tell you. Another source of her joy is clear in how her life developed in this book. That is, her long-term deep and abiding love and worship of God.

booksbybonnye.com

www.ingramcontent.com/pod-product-compliance
Lightning Source LLC
Chambersburg PA
CBHW060144150626
46550CB00014B/1345